TWENTY CYCLE RIDES IN HERTFORDSHIRE

GW00493694

St Albans / Clock Tower

Twenty Cycle Rides in Hertfordshire

Devised by
JOHN HESSION

Assisted by Members of the
Hertfordshire Wheelers/Dobsons

Illustrated by
RONALD MADDOX

Castlemead
PUBLICATIONS
WELWYN GARDEN CITY

First Published in 1989
Revised Edition April 1993

CASTLEMEAD PUBLICATIONS
12 Little Mundells
Welwyn Garden City
Herts AL7 1EW

Proprietors:
WARD'S PUBLISHING SERVICES

ISBN 0 948555 35 1

British Library Cataloguing in Publication Data
A catalogue record for this book is available from the
British Library

Set in 10/11 Ehrhardt Roman
by Input Typesetting Ltd, London SW19 8DR
Printed and bound by the Burlington Press Ltd
Foxton, Cambridge CB2 6SW

Acknowledgements

The author gratefully acknowledges the help given by the following persons and organisations in the production of this book.

John Pearson, Chairman of the Hertfordshire Wheelers, for drawing up the maps and supplying ideas.

Edgar Mascall, Club President and our oldest active member, who completed 50 years membership in 1988, for encouragement, ideas and checking of draft scripts.

Philip Young, a long-time member and his son Daniel who at 12 is our youngest member, for checking out many miles of rides on the roads.

Ronald Maddox, the artist who kindly provided the illustrations.

The Ordnance Survey for permission to use their maps as the basis for our sketch maps.

Cover photograph by Park Photographic of 52, Bullocks Lane, Hertford.

Peugeot bicycles courtesy of Graham Hicks Cycles, 89, Burford Street, Hoddesdon, Herts.

Publishers Note

Great efforts have been made to ensure that all the descriptions are accurate at the time of going to press, but the inevitable time-lag between compiling the notes and going to press, may result in some changes, especially as a result of traffic diversions and engineering works. If you encounter any problems, especially of a permanent nature, or if you have any suggestions for additions or alterations please let us know by writing to the publishers, Castlemead Publications.

Datchworth Church

Contents

Ride

Kingsbury Watermill Museum. St Michaels. St Albans

Just a Few Words About . . .

This Book
It is intended for the person who doesn't consider him or herself a committed cyclist, probably hasn't got a super lightweight bike, and who wouldn't dream of joining an official cycling club ride. In fact, it is addressed to anybody who has ever thought on a fine day 'how nice it would be to go for a bike ride in the country' but who isn't too sure how to set about it. It is also intended to be a guide for enthusiasts from outside our county who have yet to discover the wealth of quiet lanes and beautiful villages in the area.

Your Bike
The amount of enjoyment you get from cycling does not depend on the cost of your machine. Of course, experienced enthusiasts will choose light frames and equipment, but you need not delay getting out on your bike because it is not the latest and best model. Check that your tyres have no bad cuts, pump them up well, dust the machine down, make sure nothing squeaks or rattles and away you go. If you have any doubts about the condition of your machine a cycle shop which does repairs will always check it over for you.

Clothing
Cycling can make you warm – it depends on how hard you set about it. And even on a warm day you can cool off very quickly. Best advice is to wear cotton rather than man-made fibres next to your skin and to have a light jumper (or two) to put on or off so you adjust to the weather. Avoid clothing which is either too tight or too baggy. Track suits are very popular these days.

Maps
It is hoped that the descriptions and sketches are self-sufficient, but sign posts disappear or are moved, so perhaps a map would be useful. The best maps to give you more detail are the Ordnance Survey Landranger Series 1:50,000 (2 cm = 1 km, or 1.25 ins = 1 mile). Each ride gives the maps related to it. Most are on Sheet 166, Luton and Hertford.

What to Carry
It is always a good idea to have a small saddlebag and to carry a puncture repair kit and tyre levers and a pump, a set of bike spanners, a cape or kagool and headgear in case of rain and a padlock and chain. Some carry a bar of chocolate or a few boiled sweets, some money and sticking plasters, all in case of emergency. It is, of

Winter Digswell Viaduct

course, essential to carry good lamps if there is any possibility of you being out at or after dusk.

Refreshments
Don't let your ride be spoiled by your running out of energy or suffering from thirst. It is always useful to carry a bar of chocolate or a few boiled sweets and a drink, but all villages have an inn and most garden centres these days provide a snack bar and toilets.

The Rides
These have been selected to leave towns by quiet roads and to follow pleasant lanes, to afford fine views and to visit many of the more beautiful Hertfordshire villages. We have avoided busy crossings and right turns as far as possible, but some are unavoidable. And there are still plenty of other lanes and villages for you to discover.

Starting Points
All the rides start at railway stations. These can always be found and there is usually parking, especially at week-ends, for those who carry their bikes by car. Or you can take your bike on many trains (but best check first for the exceptions). With a Network card costing

only a few pounds for one year you can travel at one third off the standard fare at off-peak times (which includes all week-end) and this is certainly better than riding miles of main road before you reach the lanes.

Quiet Roads
Since all starting points are at rail stations they are generally in the centre of much road traffic. On a Sunday morning the shortest road out of town may well be free of traffic, but we have tried to suggest roads out of town and lanes in the country which are generally free of traffic, even if these are not the shortest and may involve a little walking on footpaths.

For most rides we have suggested shortened versions on quiet roads, so do take care to avoid such roads as the A10, A41, A120, etc. These are roads to be particularly avoided, but it is known that some lanes, which are quiet for most of the time, can be extremely busy at 'work' times with people trying to avoid the busy main roads!

Alternatives to These Rides
These rides do not include, or aim to include, all of the lanes and villages in the county. Having imposed constraints of using quiet roads and restricting distances to about 35 miles means that some places are not included. Readers will see that at least parts of some rides can be added to others and that detours and alternatives can be found. A word of warning, especially to inexperienced riders, would be not to be too ambitious on the early rides and to avoid some obvious short cuts such as the A class roads which bisect some of the rides. These can be highly unpleasant from the points of view of noise and fumes. Try the short cuts described and recommended.

Cycling on Canal Towpaths
Canal towpaths provide a quiet, traffic-free environment. However most of them are the property of the British Waterways Board who require cyclists to pay for a £3 annual permit. In this area the address for applications is Brindley House, Corner Hall, Lawn Lane, Hemel Hempstead; Tel. 0442 235400.

Note that on certain sections of towpath cycling is not permitted at all (notably in the Hemel Hempstead area) and that permits are issued subject to cyclists treating other towpath users with proper consideration. We are sure our readers would do this.

Points of Interest
Many places of interest are mentioned on each ride but no attempt has been made to produce a complete guide-book. With historic houses, etc. opening times and charges may vary from time to time, so these details are omitted.

Churches have not normally been mentioned unless they have a special feature, but churches are always worth a visit for architectural, historical, social and, of course, religious reasons.

Most Hertfordshire villages consist of more than one main street, so it is usually worth taking a small detour around the houses to find the odd mill stream, cricket match, Morris dancing display or garden open to the public. You can always finish the ride another time.

How Far? How Fast?

The rides in this book vary from about 15 to 35 miles. Obviously some can be linked by more ambitious riders and all can be varied to suit the day or the mood. But some readers may still have doubts about whether (say) 25 miles is a long way or not, and how long it might take. Any reasonably fit person with a mechanically sound bike should be able to cover 25 miles in half a day without any aches and pains, particularly if they are used to riding a few miles regularly. How long a ride takes you depends not so much on how fast you ride when in the saddle, as on how long you spend walking and viewing. Unless you really are pushed for time, why not allow a good half day, take it easy and enjoy the ride?

Walking up Hills

Hertfordshire has no freak hills and few difficult ones – the steepest in this book is actually on a short cut through Buckinghamshire – but you may well enjoy a break by walking up anything you find too steep or long for comfort. You can probably enjoy the scenery better by walking than by struggling. However, on a twisting road (and hills never seem to be straight) motorists, whether climbing or descending, may be surprised to find a slow-moving group of cyclist/pedestrians. So when you are walking a hill it is best to keep close to the side of the road, preferably to the right, or alternatively to the outside of the bend.

Horses

Many Hertfordshire lanes are enjoyed by horse riders as well as the rest of us. Horses have minds of their own, and however competent their riders, these animals can take fright. They may be startled by the whirring and flashing of a bicycle coming up on them closely from behind before they can hear the approach. Since bicycle bells seem to be out of fashion these days, why not give horse riders a cheerful 'Good morning' (or whatever) to let them know that you are approaching? And give the horse as wide a berth as possible.

Turning Right

Although these rides have been designed to minimise right turns, some are necessary and the right turn is a vulnerable manoeuvre for

Cromer Windmill

cyclists. You should first check over your shoulder that nobody is actually overtaking you – or has committed themselves to overtaking you. If it is clear then signal (with the hand, and not just a finger down by the hip) your intention to turn right; move to the middle of the road and when it is clear, turn. Motorists may be surprised if you stop suddenly in their paths, so, if in doubt, pull in to the side of the road, dismount and then cross.

COUNTY RIDES
KEY MAP

N

Letchworth

Hitchin • St

5

Luton

Stev

5

Harpenden

17

Tring

Sta.
19

18

16

Berkhamsted

Sta.

Sta.
St. Albans

Hemel
Hempstead

20

Radle

Sta. Watford

Rickmansworth

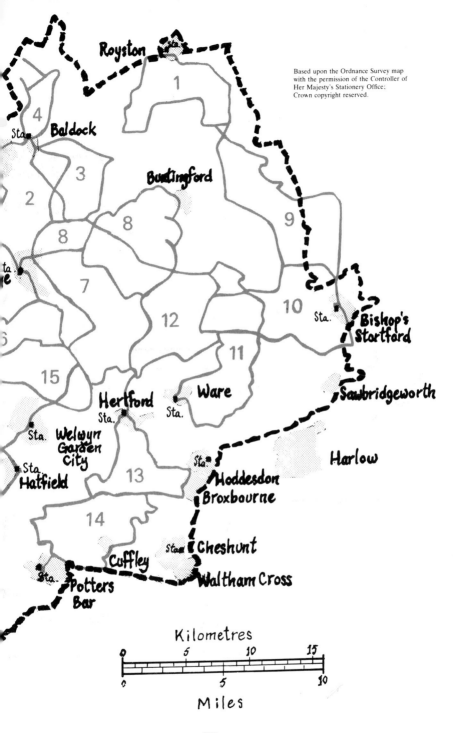

Royston

Sta.

1

4

Sta. Baldock

3

2

8

Buntingford

8

7

9

10

Sta.

Bishop's Stortford

12

11

ta. e

6

15

Ware

Sawbridgeworth

Hertford

Sta.

Sta.

Sta. Welwyn Garden City

Harlow

Sta. Hatfield

13

Sta.

Hoddesdon

Broxbourne

14

Sta. Cheshunt

Cuffley

Waltham Cross

Sta. Potters Bar

Based upon the Ordnance Survey map
with the permission of the Controller of
Her Majesty's Stationery Office;
Crown copyright reserved.

Kilometres

0   5   10   15

0   5   10

Miles

County Rides – Key to Maps

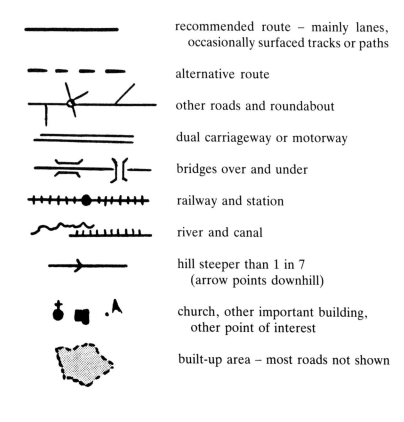

recommended route – mainly lanes, occasionally surfaced tracks or paths

alternative route

other roads and roundabout

dual carriageway or motorway

bridges over and under

railway and station

river and canal

hill steeper than 1 in 7 (arrow points downhill)

church, other important building, other point of interest

built-up area – most roads not shown

RIDE No 1

North Herts Highlands – and Fenland Views

This ride takes in some of the highest ground in the county at about 500 ft above sea level. From the village of Therfield and from near the radio mast just outside Barkway are extensive views to Cambridge and beyond. On a clear day Ely Cathedral can be seen on the horizon. These splendid views tend to overshadow the many other fine views enjoyed on this circuit.

Short cuts are suggested to avoid the A10 road on which cycling is generally not to be recommended

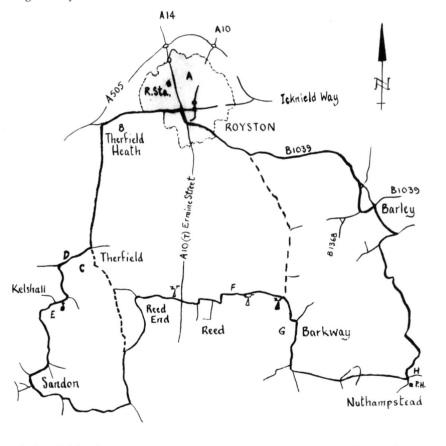

Kilometres
Miles

1

landscape near Therfield

Maps: Sheets 154 (mostly), 153, 166 (little) in the O.S. Landranger series

Based on Royston – 21 miles (alternatively 14 or 16 miles)

1   Royston to Therfield
Leave ROYSTON Station yard and turn right into Kneesworth Street to the traffic lights (**A**). Turn right into Baldock Street for 1¼ miles to Therfield turn. Turn left across Therfield Heath (**B**) and continue for 2 miles to THERFIELD.

2   Therfield to the Reed turn
Turn right on entering the village at a signpost for Kelshall(**C and D**). Follow signposts to KELSHALL (**E**) and SANDON. Follow signposts for Buckland for 1½ miles. At a T-Junction at the foot of a long descent, turn left (signposted Therfield) and then forward for 1 mile to a right junction. To the left (crossed just before the T-junction) is the infant River Rib, which rises just to the north of Reed End and flows south to Hertford to join the Lea.

3   Reed turn to Nuthampstead
Turn right at the signpost to REED. When you reach the A10 turn right and almost immediately left (*taking great care crossing the A10*).

2

Ride through Reed village and follow the signposts to BARKWAY. (**F**). At Barkway turn right onto the B1368 (**G**) and then left after ½ mile to NUTHAMPSTEAD.

4 Nuthampstead to Royston

At a T-junction at the far end of the village detour right for a short distance to the Woodman PH (**H**), then retrace and continue forward at the T-junction (signposted Barley and Royston) to MORRICE GREEN and towards Barley. At a T-junction by Putty Hall Cottages, turn right (signposted Chishills and Barley) and, after ¼ mile, turn left to BARLEY. At the village turn left to the B1368 then right at the signpost for Flint Cross. At the end of the village turn left onto the B1039 to ROYSTON. (Short Cut 2 joins from the left one mile before Royston.)

Enter Royston via Barkway Street and cross the A10 with care to Market Hill. Turn left and then right into the High Street. At the traffic lights go straight on along Kneesworth Street to the station.

Short Cuts

Note. On no account is the A10 recommended as a short cut because of its heavy volume of traffic.

Cottage at Reed

3

1   To omit 7 miles – Return to Royston via Therfield
At the end of Section 2, continue forward to THERFIELD. Continue through the village to descend via the outward route to Baldock Road. Turn right to ROYSTON.

2   To omit 5 miles – Return to Royston from near Reed
Shortly before Barkway in Section 3 (11 miles), turn left (signposted Royston) to join main ride (B1039) shortly before entering ROYSTON.

Points of Interest

A   Royston   An old market town at the crossing of Ermine Street and Icknield Way, two ancient roads. James I spent much time at Royston, hunting and shooting.
   Royston Cave, 35 ft beneath Melbourn Street, was discovered in 1742 but is of unknown origin. Measuring 30 ft by 20 ft, it is thought to be unique. Medieval wall carvings include representations of saints.
   Museum of local history, Lower King Street

B   Therfield Heath   Large open space containing pre-historic burial mounds and the only long barrow in the county

C   Therfield – Tuthill Manor   An exceptionally well restored old house not normally open to the public but visible from a lane at the side of the garden. Restored by its owner during the 1960s and 70s from almost total dereliction

D   Therfield – viewpoint   At Therfield village sign on the Kelshall road, Cambridge is easily seen, and Ely Cathedral can be seen on the skyline on a clear day. Just beyond the Kelshall turn, at a gateway, is another extensive view – the TV mast is at Sandy Heath

E   Kelshall – Church   Decorated ceiling

F   Reed – Barkway lane – viewpoint   From a point near the radio mast, Cambridge can be seen and also Ely Cathedral on a clear day

G   Barkway – High Street   Milestone bearing the arms of Trinity Hall, Cambridge. Provided from a sum of money left by Dr William Mowse, Master of Trinity Hall, who died in 1586

H   Nuthampstead – Memorial   Sited next to the Woodman PH and dedicated to US Air Force personnel who served at nearby airfield in Scales Park during World War 2

RIDE No 2

A Northern Circuit

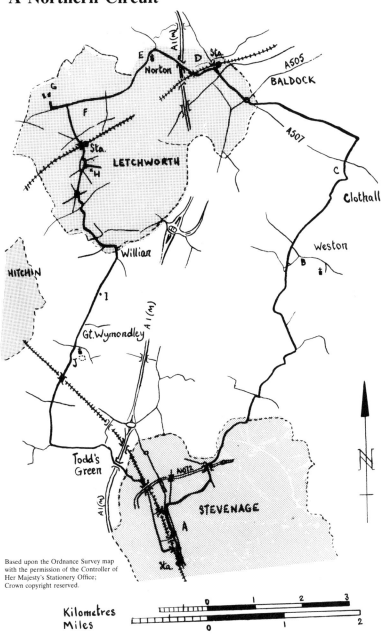

Based upon the Ordnance Survey map with the permission of the Controller of Her Majesty's Stationery Office; Crown copyright reserved.

Kilometres
Miles

Stevenage St Nicholas Church

This circuit makes a pleasant ride on its own. More than this, it links Rides 3, 4, 5, 6, 7 and 8. This means that riders from Stevenage, Baldock, Letchworth and Hitchin can link into any of these rides and avoid the roads A505, A507, A602 and A6141 which generally carry too much heavy traffic to permit pleasant cycling.

Map: Sheet 166 in the O.S. Landranger series

Based on Stevenage, Baldock, Letchworth or Hitchin – 20 miles

1   Stevenage to Weston

From STEVENAGE Station (**A**) car park descend to the cycleway between the car park and the rail track. Turn right (northwards) and descend to a junction. Turn left and then right to follow signs to Old Town, alongside and then under Lytton Way, and then sharp left. Beyond a lorry park on the right turn right, via Drapers Way to reach the High Street. Turn left and soon (just before the one-way system) right into Walkern Road. At the end turn left into Almonds Lane to St Nicholas' Church, and then right into Weston Road. Where the old road ends turn left on a new estate road for ¼ mile. At the roundabout turn right for WESTON (**B**).

2   Weston to Baldock

At Weston pond continue forward to CLOTHALL, taking care on the descent through the village. Just beyond a double bend at the foot of the hill, on the left is the church (**C**). Cross the A507 with care, continue forward via a narrow lane past Quickswood, to rejoin the A507 near Baldock (**D**). Turn right onto the A507. At a roundabout take the second exit and follow Clothall Road to cross the A505 at the traffic lights. BALDOCK station is soon on the right.

3   Baldock to Letchworth
Turn left opposite the station into Icknield Way. At the end, turn right and ride for ½ mile down Norton Road. At the T-junction turn left and ride through NORTON village (**E**) to enter LETCH-WORTH via Norton Road. At a roundabout take the second exit along Wilbury Road for ½ mile (**F**). Standalone Farm (**G**) is on the right, just beyond a sharp descent. If you are not visiting the farm turn left, *BEFORE* the descent in Wilbury Road, down Cowslip Hill and climb to Icknield Way. Cross to Bridge Road, go over the rail bridge, and bear left to Letchworth Station (**H**).

4   Letchworth to Redcoats Green
At the roundabout outside the station turn right into Broadway, and ride via Town Square (John F. Kennedy Gardens) continue along Broadway past St Francis College. (*Take care in the one-way system – walking through the gardens may be more pleasant if traffic is heavy.*) At a small roundabout take the second exit – Spring Road. At the end of this road cross the A505 and immediately turn left into Letchworth Lane. Descend (*taking care at the sharp lefthand bend at the bottom*) and continue to a T-junction. Turn left to WILLIAN.

On entering the village, opposite the pond, turn right with care at a double junction. Go straight on for 1 mile (**I**) to GREAT WYMONDLEY (**J**). Note the very old houses on either side of the road into this village.

A quiet way to and from Hitchin, for rides other than No 5, joins here. (*See* Section 7 below.)

At Great Wymondley crossroads continue forward to descend to a roundabout on the A602. Go straight over to climb past the Blakemore Hotel to a T-junction by Redcoats Farm Hotel. (*To join Ride No 5 from here see Section 6 below.*)

5   Redcoats Green to Stevenage
Turn left. (The signpost to Stevenage is hidden in the hedge.) Carry on through TITMORE GREEN and TODDS GREEN to FISHERS GREEN. Soon after crossing the motorway bridge turn left into Fishers Green Road which later becomes Fairview Road. After 1½ miles, just before a junction with Gunnels Wood Road, join the cycleway on the right. Descend to a T-junction, and here turn left

onto another cycleway. Just after passing under the rail bridge turn right to STEVENAGE station.

6   To join Ride No 5 from Redcoats Green

Turn right at Redcoats Green Farmhouse. Just past the village sign for St Ippollitts and before a descent, turn right into the village. Bear left past the church, and follow Ride No 5 from Section 6, the alternative quiet route to Charlton.

7   A quiet link into this circuit, to and from Hitchin, for rides other than No 5

Follow Ride No 5, Section 6 (the alternative quiet route out of Hitchin) as far as Wymondley Road, and then continue forward to reach GREAT WYMONDLEY. On return, leave Wymondley in the direction of HITCHIN and shortly after the rail bridge, turn right into Halsey Drive. Follow Ride No 5, Section 5 to Hitchin station.

REVERSE DIRECTION

5   Stevenage Station to Redcoats Green

From STEVENAGE Station car park descend to the cycleway between the car park and the rail track. Turn right (northwards) and, after an underpass, sharp left (signposted 'Gunnels Wood Road') under the railway. Take the first cycleway on the right to Fairview Road. You will soon leave the cycleway system. Go forward in Fairview Road, which becomes Fishers Green Road, for 1½ miles. At the end of this turn right via TODDS GREEN to REDCOATS GREEN. (*To join Ride No 5 turn left to St Ippollitts and follow Section 6 above.*)

4   Redcoats Green to Letchworth

At the lefthand bend by Redcoats Green Farmhouse turn right. Descend to the roundabout on the A602, and continue forward to GREAT WYMONDLEY (**J**). At the crossroads note the old houses on both sides of the road, continuing forward to WILLIAN (**I**). On entering the village turn left and then left again. After a short climb, turn right and ride on past Letchworth Hall Hotel, to enter LETCH-WORTH (**H**). At the A505 turn right and immediately left into Spring Road. Soon, at a small roundabout take the fourth exit (Broadway) and continue forward, via Town Square, (John F. Kennedy Gardens) to the roundabout opposite Letchworth Station.

3   Letchworth to Baldock

Turn left and follow the road round to the right to cross the rail bridge and descend to Icknield Way. At the roundabout take the second exit (Cowslip Hill) and descend. If you are visiting Standalone Farm (**G**), turn left into Longmead and at the end turn left into

Wilbury Road – the farm is a little way on the right. If not visiting the farm continue forward up Cowslip Hill and at the top turn right into Wilbury Road. Continue forward past Norton Common on the right. At a small roundabout take the second exit (Norton Road) to NORTON village (**E**). Beyond the village turn right along Norton Road to BALDOCK (**D**). Just after passing under the rail bridge, turn left into Icknield Way. At the end (Station Road, A507) is Baldock Station.

2 Baldock to Weston

Turn right onto A507 as far as the traffic lights on the A505. Carry on forward along Clothall Road for ½ mile to a roundabout where continue forward for 200 yards. Look out for a left turn into an unsignposted lane opposite Cambrai Farm. Follow this lane for 1½ miles, past Quickswood to re-emerge on the A507. Cross with care into a lane and soon on the right, just past the old School House is Clothall Church (**C**). Continue through the village to WESTON (**B**).

1 Weston to Stevenage

At Weston pond continue straight on to enter STEVENAGE. Turn left on a new estate road, and after ¼ mile take a footpath on the right to lead through to the old road to the T-junction by St Nicholas' Church. Here turn left into Almonds Lane and soon right into Walkern Road, at the end of which turn left into the High Street. Soon, at the narrow part of the High Street, turn right into Drapers Way. Just beyond a lorry park on the left, turn left onto a cycleway alongside Lytton Way. At a T-junction turn right under Lytton Way and then left. After ¼ mile, turn left and then right on the cycleway to the station.

Points of Interest

A Stevenage First of the New Towns to be designated after World War 2. Noted for its well designed and safe cycleway system and pedestrian Town Centre. Museum in St George's Way

Weston

B Weston Arguably one of the prettiest villages in the county. See the note under Ride No 3 regarding the giant's grave in the churchyard, which is a detour from this ride, but worth making

C Clothall The surprising view from the gate at the back of the churchyard is worth seeing. Note on the side of a hill on the other side of the A507 some terracing (lynchets), signs of an ancient form of cultivation

D Baldock Built by the Knights Templars at the crossing of three Roman (or older) roads about 1140. Many traces of Roman occupation have been found, notably to the east of the town. Some of these are on view in Letchworth Museum.
   The wide High Street reminds us of the time when it was a coaching town before the railway came. It runs parallel to Clothall Road, and may be too busy with traffic for cycling but is worth a visit. At the south end the modern Tesco store is behind the facade of the former stocking factory which was built as a film studio but which never made a film. Just beyond the north end of the High Street is the George and Dragon, a fine example of a coaching inn, although the courtyard is now covered to form a dining room

E Norton Church of Norman origin, and a pre-Norman village which has just avoided being absorbed into Letchworth Garden City

F Norton Common Large open space. Cycling is not permitted but a walk of ¼ mile across to Icknield Way, Quadrant and to Bridge Road may make a welcome break

G Standalone Farm Working farm with cattle, sheep, pigs and poultry. Open to visitors in summer. Exhibitions of natural history and farm machinery

H Letchworth Garden City The first Garden City, founded in 1904. Noted for its tree-lined roads.
   Museum of archaeology and natural history in Town Square.
   First Garden City Heritage Museum in Norton Way South records history of the Garden City movement and social history of Letchworth.
   Leys Avenue, The Letchworth Shop. Tourist Information Centre

I Memorial on roadside ½ mile from Willian, commemorating death in a crash nearby during a flying exercise in 1912 of two officers of the Royal Flying Corps – pioneers, indeed

J Great Wymondley – churchyard Motte and bailey (12th century) lie on the boundary of the churchyard. Those interested in ley lines may care to note that this church, St Mary's, Hitchin, and those at Graveley and Chesfield are in a direct line

RIDE No 3

More North Herts Highlands

This ride contains many extensive views from some of the highest ground in the county, although it contains no excessively steep hills. It includes fine old villages and a giant's grave. At Sandon this ride can be linked to Ride No 1, based on Royston, even if only to include the loop around Therfield and to enjoy the views from near that village.

The A507 road is not generally to be recommended as a short cut on this ride. As a road it is very pleasant but it often carries a heavy volume of traffic, making cycling unpleasant

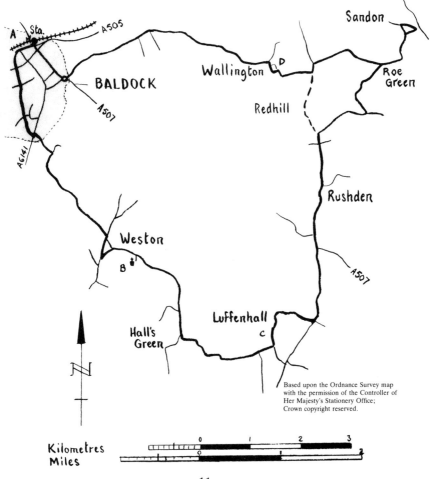

Based upon the Ordnance Survey map
with the permission of the Controller of
Her Majesty's Stationery Office;
Crown copyright reserved.

Kilometres
Miles

11

Old Post Office/Row Weston

Maps: Sheets 153 and 166 in the O.S. Landranger series

Based on Baldock – 18 miles (alternatively 15 miles)
Alternatively, using Ride No 2 – from Letchworth – add 6 miles;
from Hitchin – add 16 miles; or from Stevenage – add 10 miles

1 Baldock to Weston

Leave BALDOCK Station (**A**), cross Station Road (A507) and ride
into Icknield Way. At the end bear left into Norton Road to its end.
Cross Hitchin Street (A505) with care and forward into Weston Way.
At the end turn left onto the A6141 and soon right up a hill through
beech trees to WESTON (**B**).

2 Weston to Sandon turn

Turn right, and at the pond turn left (signposted Halls Green,
Cromer) and riding through HALLS GREEN and on for a mile to
a gentle descent. Where the road bends right (signposted Walkern),

farm at Luffenhall

continue straight on (signposted Cromer) down a steep narrow lane to LUFFENHALL (**C**).

Turn left at the foot of the hill and follow signs to RUSHDEN until a sign pointing right 'Rushden, Southern Green'. Here, go straight on, past the Moon and Stars PH, to a turning on the right signposted to Sandon and Kelshall.

3 To Sandon and the Wallington turn

Here, turn right to ROE GREEN, and then turn right again towards Sandon. At a right bend near Sandon Saddlery go straight on and then bear right to rejoin the road again by SANDON pond. (*Ride No 1 can be joined here.*)

Retrace to ROE GREEN, and then at the recreation ground continue forward (signposted Wallington) for a mile, to descend to a T-junction. Here turn left for a short distance to a righthand turn signposted 'Wallington'.

4 Wallington turn to Baldock

Turn right to WALLINGTON (**D**) with fine views to the right. Take care on the bends through the village and continue forward for three miles to BALDOCK and the roundabout on the A507. Take the third exit (Clothall Road) to the traffic lights on the A505, then go straight on along Station Road to the station.

Short cut to omit 3 miles

From Sandon turn to Wallington
At the end of Section 2 continue forward to a left turn to WALLING-TON to rejoin the main ride at Section 4.

Points of Interest

A Baldock See note under Ride No 2

B Weston One of the finest villages in the county. Weston Church-yard – half a mile from the village centre, at the foot of a gentle descent and just past Oakleys Farm on the left, turn into the lane on the right. Just inside the churchyard, on the left, is the grave of Jack o'Legs. This legendary giant, a local Robin Hood, is said to have taken bread from the bakers of Baldock to give to the poor. When he was caught his eyes were put out and he was condemned to death. It was decreed that he should be buried where landed an arrow shot from his bow. Fired from Jack's Hill on the Great North Road, the arrow landed in Weston Churchyard

C Luffenhall Hamlet consists of a beautiful collection of thatched and pargetted cottages

D Wallington George Orwell, the writer, lived here in the 1930s

13

RIDE No 4

Some Ancient North Herts Villages

A ride amongst ancient villages, churches and houses and a pond 1000 years old

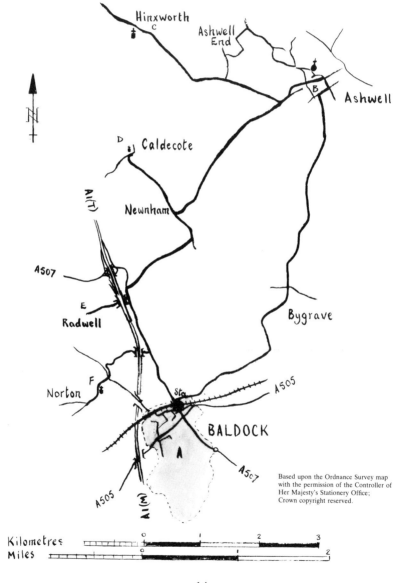

Based upon the Ordnance Survey map with the permission of the Controller of Her Majesty's Stationery Office; Crown copyright reserved.

14

Map: Sheet 153 in the O.S. Landranger series

Based on Baldock – 18 miles
Alternatively, using Ride No 2, from Letchworth – 24 miles; Hitchin – 34 miles; or Stevenage – 36 miles

1 Baldock to Ashwell

From BALDOCK Station yard (**A**) turn right onto North Road (A507) and after 100 yards right again for 4 miles, through BYGRAVE to ASHWELL. Entering the village down hill, turn left at a T-junction (signposted Newnham, Hinxworth) and continue downhill through a narrow lane (marked 'unsuitable for wide vehicles') to the High Street. There is much to see in Ashwell (**B**).

2 Ashwell to Hinxworth

Leave Ashwell via Gardiners Lane, (opposite the lane by which we entered the High Street), bearing left twice on leaving the village, to ASHWELL END. At Bluegates Farm (T-junction) turn left to Hinxworth Road, and then turn right to HINXWORTH (**C**).

3 Hinxworth to Caldecote

Return to ASHWELL, using the direct route. On entering the village, turn sharp right and ride over the hill (passing on the left, as we climb the hill, Arbury Banks, an Iron Age settlement) to NEWNHAM. At the end of Newnham turn right for ¾ mile to CALDECOTE (**D**).

5 Caldecote to Radwell

Retrace to NEWNHAM and then go straight on (signposted Baldock). Turn left onto the A507 (*with care*) and soon right to RADWELL. Descend through the village and at the end of the surfaced road you will see Radwell Mill (**E**) across a large lake with many ducks.

6 Radwell to Baldock

Return to the A507 and carefully turn right for ¾ mile (*if traffic is heavy, use the footpath*) and as the road descends, turn right again (no signpost) into Norton Bury Lane. This lane twists for ¾ mile to a T-junction where turn left to emerge at a junction by a 'Letchworth' sign. Take Norton Road (signposted Letchworth) to NORTON village (**F**). Retrace to the junction and now turn right to BALDOCK. On entering Baldock (under the rail bridge) turn left into Icknield Way to emerge on Station Road (A507) opposite the station.

Points of Interest

A Baldock An interesting and historic town. See note under Ride No 2

B Ashwell One of the finest of all Herts villages, dating from Roman times. Has been described as 'the most unspoilt village in England'. See the springs, source of the River Rhee or Cam; the village museum in a Tudor Tithe Office; restored Foresters' Cottages; carvings on a wall in the church from 1350, time of the Black Death

C Hinxworth Most northerly village in Hertfordshire; many picturesque cottages; association with writer Monica Dickens who lived and wrote here. *My turn to make the tea* describes her experiences working on a local newspaper

D Caldecote Church (now maintained by the Redundant Churches Fund) where village has disappeared over time. Some sixty sites in the county are thought to be former villages which have been abandoned

E Radwell Mill pond which has existed since Domesday. Try counting the ducks, who will expect some food from you

F Norton Norman Church and pre-Norman village which is not quite absorbed into Letchworth Garden City

RIDE No 5

North Central Herts
– And The Source of Two Rivers

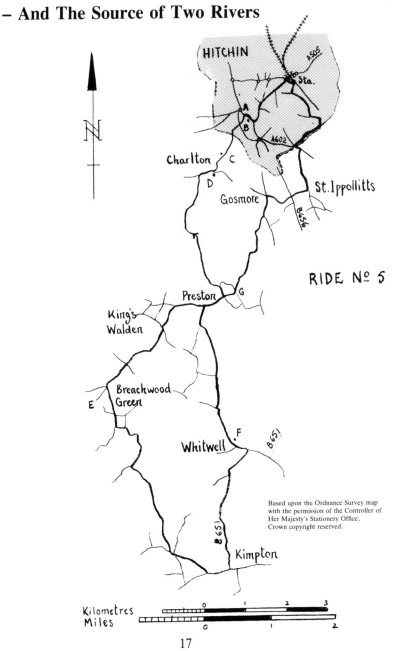

Based upon the Ordnance Survey map with the permission of the Controller of Her Majesty's Stationery Office; Crown copyright reserved.

A gently hilly circuit with some excellent valley views and two river sources. The Hiz flows through Hitchin and thence to the Bedfordshire Ouse and the North Sea via the Wash. A few miles away the Mimram starts and joins the Lea at Hertford and flows thence to the North Sea via the Thames. We can see the watercress beds on the Mimram and buy fresh cress at Whitwell. En route we look down on the runway of Luton International Airport

Map: Sheet 166 in the O.S. Landranger series

Based on Hitchin – 20 miles (alternatively 10 or 15 miles)
Alternatively, using Ride No 2, from Baldock – add 16 miles; Letchworth – add 8 miles; or Stevenage – add 7 miles

1 Hitchin to Charlton
From HITCHIN Station yard (**A**), turn left into Walsworth Road for ½ mile. Go straight on at the traffic lights along Queen Street. (*If traffic is heavy in Walsworth Road take the quieter route, see Section 6 below.*) At the end of Queen Street, at a roundabout by the Lord Lister Hotel, take the second exit (Bridge Street) (**B**) which becomes Tilehouse Street. Halfway up turn left into Old Charlton Road. At the end cross the bypass via the underpass. Beyond the underpass, turn left and then right into Charlton Road. After ¼ mile turn left to CHARLTON (**C**). Ride through the village for ¼ mile to a lane joining from the left (**D**).

Hitchin Tilehouse Street

2 Charlton to Kings Walden

Continue forward passing the Water Company pumping station on your right, until you reach a lane ahead marked 'no through road'. Here bear sharp left, then forward for 2 miles to PRESTON. On entering this village, turn right into Butchers Lane and at an unsignposted crossroads turn right again to follow signposts to KINGS WALDEN. Ride through the village (*taking care on the downhill bend*) and continue to a crossroads.

3 Kings Walden to Kimpton and Whitwell

Continue forward to BREACHWOOD GREEN. As you climb the hill note the view down the Mimram valley to the left; the river source is 1½ miles away. On entering the village turn left into Heath Road and then forward to the far end, beyond a childrens playground on the left (**E**). Turn left and follow the signposts to Kimpton for a nice (mainly) downhill run of 3 miles.

On entering KIMPTON turn left into the High Street and at the far end of the village turn left (Hitchin Road, B651) to Whitwell. Take care on the descent to this village. At the T-junction at the foot of the hill in WHITWELL turn left (**F**).

4 Whitwell to St Ippollytts

Continue through the village for nearly a mile, to a point just beyond a lefthand bend by Stagenhoe Bottom Farm where an unsigned lane leaves to the right. Turn right and continue forward to a T-junction where turn right again to PRESTON (**G**). In the centre of the village turn left, signposted Hitchin, to Gosmore. In GOSMORE turn right at the Bull PH and cross over the B656 to ST IPPOLLYTTS.

5 St Ippollytts to Hitchin

Opposite the church, turn left, signposted Hitchin, to emerge on the A602. Turn left and after ¼ mile right into Whitehill Road. Almost immediately turn right again into Oakfield Avenue. At the end by the Fountain PH, turn right into Ninesprings Way, to Wymondley Road. Turn left and soon right into Halsey Drive and near the top turn right into Stuart Drive. At the end, by a school, continue forward via a footpath. Follow the path to the right and then left into Benslow Lane. At the beginning of a descent turn right into Benslow Rise; follow round a lefthand bend and to the bottom, and there keep going on a footpath. At a junction, turn right to emerge at Hitchin Station.

6 Alternative quiet route from Hitchin to Charlton

At the exit from the station car park to Walsworth Road take a footpath on the left. After a short distance, turn left again to emerge in Benslow Rise. Turn right to a T-junction where turn left into Benslow Lane to the top of the hill. Continue forward via a footpath to a T-junction where turn right to follow the path round a school field and emerge in Stuart Drive. Go on and at the end turn left into Halsey Drive. Descend to Wymondley Road; turn left in Wymondley Road and soon turn right again into Ninesprings Way. Soon (opposite the Fountain PH) turn left into Oakfield Avenue. At the end turn left and left again onto the A602. Soon turn right to ST IPPOLLYTTS. In the village turn right to descend to a crossroads on the B656. Go straight over along Waterdell Lane to GOSMORE. At the Bull PH go forward in Maydencroft Lane (*care, horses*) to descend to CHARLTON. Either turn left to follow the main ride or detour a mile or so to the right to see Hitchin Priory (**B**), Tilehouse Street, etc.

Short Cuts

1   To omit 10 miles – From Preston to Hitchin
At PRESTON the first time (in Section 2), turn left at the unsign-posted crossroads to the village and read from Section 4.

2   To omit 5 miles – Kings Walden to the Preston turn
At the crossroads beyond KINGS WALDEN, (the end of Section 2), turn left towards Whitwell for 2 miles, to an unsignposted turn on the left. Turn left to join the main ride at Section 4.

Points of Interest

A   Hitchin Market town. Museum of local history and regimental museum of Hertfordshire Yeomanry in Paynes Park in the middle of a one-way system. Best approached from the top of Tilehouse Street if traffic is heavy. Tourist information centre at museum

B   Hitchin – The Priory, Tilehouse Street Former monastic house, later home of the Delme-Radcliffe family for 300 years. Now offices of an insurance company

C   Charlton A plaque on the house opposite the Windmill PH com-memorates the birthplace of Sir Henry Bessemer, inventor of the steel-making process named after him

D   Charlton The source of the River Hiz is in a field on the left by the lane junction

E   Breachwood Green A distant view of the runway of Luton Air-port. Mind your head when jets are landing!

F   Whitwell Watercress beds and the chance to buy freshly cut cress

G   Preston Many picturesque old cottages. The Red Lion PH is owned by the villagers. John Bunyan, nonconformist preacher, was active in this area

RIDE No 6

The Mimram Valley

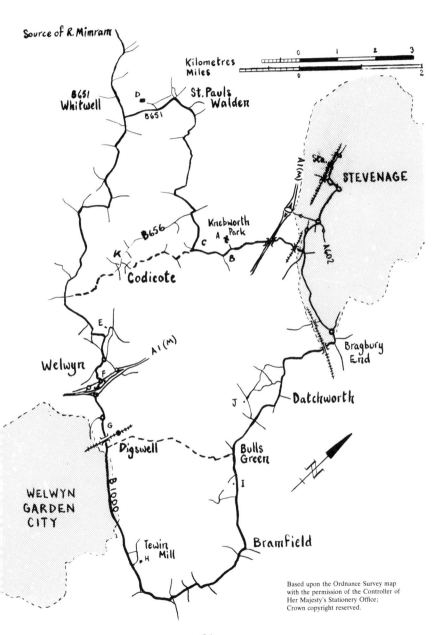

Source of R. Mimram

Kilometres
Miles

0   1   2   3
0   2

B651
Whitwell

D

B651

St. Pauls
Walden

A1(M)

Sta.

STEVENAGE

B656

Knebworth
Park

A   C

B

K

A602

Codicote

E

A1(M)

Welwyn

F

Bragbury
End

J

Datchworth

G

Digswell

Bulls
Green

I

WELWYN
GARDEN
CITY

B1000

Tewin
Mill

H

Bramfield

21

This ride follows leafy lanes to the source of the River Mimram (or Maran) near Whitwell. It then traces the river to a point near its junction with the Lea at Hertford, returning through more pleasant wooded lanes. On the way we find watercress beds, a Roman Bath House under the A1(M), some industrial archaeology, and the spot where a highwayman was put to death

Map: Sheet 166 in the O.S. Landranger series

Based on Stevenage – 30 miles (alternatively 26, 22 or 18 miles)
Alternatively, using Ride No 2, from Baldock – add 18 miles; Letchworth – add 16 miles; or Hitchin – add 14 miles
From Hertford – 30 or 22 miles; or Welwyn Garden City – 29 or 21 miles

1   Stevenage to The Roebuck Inn

From STEVENAGE Station descend to the cycle track between the car park and the rail lines, turn left (southwards) and soon at a crosstrack, left again for ¼ mile past a 'Police' sign and the County Library. Opposite a duck pond (on the left) turn right via an underpass signposted 'Shephall, Broadwater' and 'Stevenage College'. Beyond the underpass turn left again and forward. After ½ mile take care crossing a car park entrance/exit (**A**). Just beyond this turn left, and immediately after a 2nd underpass, right (signed 'The Roebuck'). The cycleway emerges on Roebuck Gate. Cross Hertford Road to the Roebuck Inn.

2   The Roebuck to St Pauls Walden

At the Roebuck Inn cross London Road (B197) and enter Old Knebworth Lane to OLD KNEBWORTH. Turn right (signposted Codicote) for ½ mile (**B**) to NUP END. Turn right and immediately right again (signposted Hitchin). Take care not to miss the second right turn. Continue forward for ½ mile (**C**) to the B656. Here turn right and almost immediately left into Three Houses Lane. After ½ mile turn right and use the twisting lane to ST PAULS WALDEN (**D**).

3   St Pauls Walden to Welwyn

Turn left onto the B651 to a T-junction at WHITWELL. The source of the Mimram is about 1½ miles to the right, through Whitwell, towards Lilley, on the left of the road, just beyond Stagenhoe Bottom Farm. Return through Whitwell and proceed towards Codicote until 1½ miles beyond Whitwell. Here, shortly after passing Crouch Green Lane on the left, turn right into a narrow unsigned lane to descend to KIMPTON MILL. Here the Mimram gurgles merrily under the road after passing through some watercress beds. Turn left to follow the river for nearly 2 miles to the next crossroads.

Welwyn / Church Street

Keep straight on towards Welwyn, with the river still close on your left. After climbing a steep hill, turn left into Oakhill Drive, a private road. At the end turn right into Fulling Mill Lane (**E**), to rejoin Kimpton Road and then emerge on Codicote Road to enter WELWYN.

4 Welwyn to Bramfield turn

Walk the one-way street to the right to enter the High Street, and soon after crossing the river, turn left at the White Hart Inn. Keep on the A1000 under a road bridge (**F**), and continue forward on the A1000 (*taking care at a motorway exit*) and then the B1000 to cross the Mimram yet again; here you have an excellent view of Digswell Viaduct (**G**). Keep straight on to DIGSWELL.

Continue on the B1000 for 3½ miles towards Hertford (**H**). After crossing the river (which now passes through a private estate before joining the Lea), climb a hill, to a left turn.

5 Bramfield turn to The Roebuck Inn

Turn left and then forward to BRAMFIELD, enjoying some fine views from the road, then keeping left through the village (**I**), straight on through BULLS GREEN and DATCHWORTH GREEN (**J**). Continue forward to DATCHWORTH and BRAGBURY END. At a garden centre join the cycleway and almost immediately turn left alongside the A602. Soon turn left to Blenheim Way. Here leave the cycleway, turn right into Hertford Road and then turn left. At the roundabout go straight on (signposted 'No through road') and continue to the Roebuck Inn.

6 The Roebuck to Stevenage

Turn right into Roebuck Gate and immediately on the left join the cycleway alongside the B197 (London Road). Just past the football ground turn left at a T-junction, (signposted 'Gunnels Wood, Town Centre'). Immediately after the second underpass turn right and keep forward towards the Town Centre. (*Take care crossing the car park entrance and exit.*) Just after the cycleway bears left near the college, turn right under the road and then left (signposted 'Town Centre'), past the 'County Library' and 'Police Station' signs and soon turn right to the railway station.

Short Cuts

1 To omit 8 miles – From Nup End to Welwyn
At NUP END (in Section 2) keep forward to CODICOTE (**K**), where turn left on the B656 and soon take the second right (signposted Wheathampstead). At the crossroads at the foot of the hill, turn left towards WELWYN to join the main ride in Section 3.

2 To omit 4 miles – From Digswell to Bulls Green
After the viaduct (in Section 4) turn left into Harmer Green Lane and climb up the hill to HARMER GREEN. Keep on round the green and forward to BURNHAM GREEN and BULLS GREEN where turn left to join the main ride in Section 5.

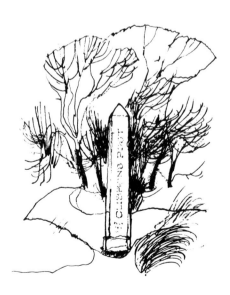

Bulls Green - Guttons Post

Alternative start and finish points

1 Hertford North Station – 30 or 22 miles
Start
Turn left from HERTFORD NORTH Station on North Road (A119) for ¹/₂ mile. At the cemetery turn left to BRAMFIELD. Join the main ride at Section 5.

To omit Stevenage
At the Roebuck Inn (end of Section 5) read the main ride from Section 2.

Finish
From the end of Section 4 follow the B1000 to Hertford.

2 Welwyn Garden City – 29 or 21 miles
Start
From the front of WELWYN GARDEN CITY Station turn right along Stonehills to a roundabout where take the third exit into Bridge Road (B195). Cross the rail bridge to a roundabout where turn left into Bessemer Road. After ½ mile, at a one-way system take the second exit to the B1000 via Waterside. (*Better to use the cycleway on the left just before the one-way system. A somewhat complicated but well signposted route leads to Waterside.*) Descend to a T-junction where turn right towards Hertford, and join the main ride in Section 4.

To omit Stevenage
At the Roebuck Inn (end of Section 5) read the main ride from Section 2.

Finish
After Welwyn, at the Digswell roundabout and in sight of the railway viaduct, turn right (A1000). Soon turn right again into Digswell Road and over the hill to The Campus. Turn left and at Bridge Road left again and almost immediately right into Stonehills to the station.

3 Welwyn North Station
Start
Turn right out of WELWYN NORTH Station and descend Harmer Green Lane. At the bottom turn left onto the B1000 towards Hertford to join the main ride in Section 4.

To omit Stevenage
At the Roebuck Inn (end of Section 5), read the main ride from Section 2.

Finish
Just before the viaduct turn left at 'Station' sign.

25

Points of Interest

A   Knebworth House and Park   Tudor mansion ½ mile from car park – to the right, off the A1(M) roundabout. Currently home of the Hon. David Lytton Cobbold. During the 19th century home of the novelist, Bulwer Lytton. House, gardens and grounds open to public.

B   Old Knebworth Forge   Usually open at weekends

C   Knebworth Park   Viewed on the right may offer a glimpse of a herd of deer

D   St Pauls Walden Bury   Childhood home of Queen Elizabeth, the Queen Mother. Gardens occasionally open in summer

E   Welwyn – Fulling-mill   A short detour to the left is a fulling-mill (no longer in action). Fulling, a process involving water and fuller's earth, was used from the 12th to 17th century to cleanse and tighten the weave of newly woven woollen cloth. The present mill is not so old

F   Welwyn – Roman bath house   Either ride the A1000 around the roundabout, or walk the one-way section under the bridge and along the slip road from the roundabout to see the Roman bath house; preserved under the A1(M), this was featured in the BBC *Timewatch* series on archaeology

G   Digswell Viaduct   Built in 1850 by Lewis Cubitt for the Great Northern Railway, from bricks made on the site, the viaduct carries the East Coast Main Line from London to Scotland 100 feet above the Mimram Valley on fifty arches – try counting them! It is 1560 feet long

H   Tewin – Hydraulic pump   The ruin of a hydraulic pump can be seen soon after Tewin Mill House, by a footbridge on the left signposted 'Footpath to Tewin'

I   Bramfield – Clibbons Post   One and a half miles beyond the village, on the left, soon after the Bramfield Forest car park and a dip in the lane is a post, erected in 1927 by the East Herts. Archaeological Society. It marks the spot where local men dealt with Walter Clibbon, highwayman in 1782. He was done to death and buried with a stake through his heart to prevent him doing further mischief. The gun which was used to shoot him is in Hertford Museum.

J   Datchworth Green   A short way to the left from the crossroads, on the left, is a whipping post

K   Codicote   An old, pre-Norman village site with many old buildings to be seen, although there has been much recent development

RIDE No 7

The Beane Valley

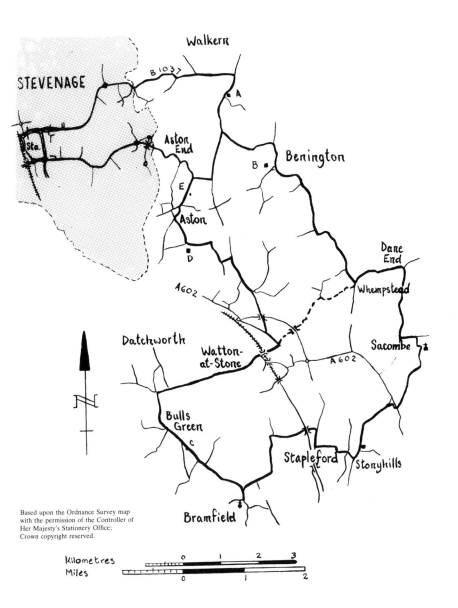

Based upon the Ordnance Survey map
with the permission of the Controller of
Her Majesty's Stationery Office;
Crown copyright reserved.

This ride is easy pedalling, following the course of the River Beane from Walkern Mill, not far from its source, towards Hertford, where it joins the Lea. We encounter some high, open ground with distant views to start with and some wooded lanes near Bramfield and Datchworth on the return. In addition to the river we can see a Norman castle, a highwayman's grave and a farm open to visitors

Map: Sheet 166 in the O.S. Landranger series

Based on Stevenage – 28 miles (alternatively 18 miles)
Alternatively, using Ride No 2, from Baldock – add 18 miles; Letchworth – add 16 miles; or Hitchin – add 14 miles
Also from Hertford – 23 miles

1   Stevenage Station to Walkern
From STEVENAGE Station descend to the cycleway between the car park and the rail track. Turn right (northwards) and descend through the first underpass. At a T-junction, turn right (signposted 'All areas except Gunnels Wood') and forward along the cycleway alongside Fairlands Way. Take care crossing Popple Way (*only interruption on 2 miles of cycleway*) and keep going until cycleway ends near a school. Join the road on the right (Walkern Road, B1037) and continue in the same direction until you reach WALKERN.

Bennington Village Green

2   Walkern to Stonyhills

At a T-junction turn right (signposted Benington, Watton), and at the end of the village cross the river at Walkern Mill (**A**). After a mile turn left to BENINGTON (**B**). Bear left at the pond in the village and forward for 2½ miles to WHEMPSTEAD.

At the crossroads turn left to descend to DANE END, where at a T-junction turn right for 1½ miles, to SACOMBE. Turn left in the village (signposted 'Sacombe Green') and soon right to Sacombe Church. Beyond the church keep forward on the bridleway. This is stony but rideable for a short way, but beyond a farm it runs along a driveway. Keep forward to the A602. Cross this road, with care, and turn half right for a mile to STONYHILLS, the Three Harts PH.

3   Stonyhills to Watton-at-Stone

Soon after the Three Harts, turn right and soon take care on a lefthand bend, to descend a steep, narrow lane to STAPLEFORD. Here note the unusual 19th century bell tower on a church with two Norman doorways. Turn right onto the A119 for ½ mile, then turn left, just beyond the Woodhall Arms, to BRAMFIELD. The village lays to the left and is worth a short detour. Our ride is to the right (**C**) to BULLS GREEN and DATCHWORTH GREEN. At the crossroads turn right for 2½ miles to WATTON-AT-STONE.

4   Watton to Aston End

In the village, at the pump, turn left into the main street. At the end of the village turn right towards WALKERN. After 1¼ miles, after descending a hill, turn left, via ASTON BURY (**D**) to ASTON. Leave Aston via New Park Lane rather than Aston End Road. This is to the right, and then left at the bottom of Stringers Lane, which is to the right as the village is entered. Keep straight on in New Park Lane (**E**) to a junction on the right near Aston End.

5   Aston End to Stevenage

Continue forward (signposted Aston End) and then right into Long Lane, and soon fork left to Poplars Farm. Keep straight on (signposted 'No through road') via an underpass to join a footpath/cycleway. Turn right on a short, poorly surfaced section to a roundabout. Turn left onto the cycleway alongside Six Hills Way for 2 miles towards the town centre. Shortly beyond 'County Library' and 'Police Station' signs, turn right to STEVENAGE Station.

Short cut to omit 10 miles – Whempstead to Watton-at-Stone
At WHEMPSTEAD in Section 2, turn right (signposted Watton) and continue forward to descend to the Watton Bypass. Cross with care and keep forward on a surfaced bridleway to WATTON High Street. Here turn right to join the main ride at Section 4.

Alternative start and finish

Hertford North Station – distance 23 miles

Start

Turn left on leaving HERTFORD NORTH Station yard, into North Road (A119), signposted Stevenage, for ½ mile. At the cemetery, turn left to BRAMFIELD where turn right to join the main ride in Section 3.

To omit Stevenage

At the end of Section 4, near Aston End, turn right (signposted Watton) to descend through a ford and then climb to the Watton-Walkern road. Turn left for a mile, then sharp right to BENING-TON. Join main ride in Section 2.

Finish

At the end of Section 2, continue beyond the Three Harts to BENGEO. Descend Port Hill with care. At the bottom turn right into Port Vale and continue forward, using the footpath through to Molewood Road. At the end turn left in Beane Road to HERT-FORD NORTH Station.

Alternatively, descend to STAPLEFORD to make a decision regarding traffic on the A119 road. If this is not too heavy, the road into Hertford affords many pleasant views of the Beane and passes the station.

Points of Interest

A *Walkern Mill* Recently restored and converted for private use, this building is at the south end of the village where the road crosses the river. This mill is not open to the public

B *Benington Lordship* Norman keep, Victorian folly and gardens open to the public on Sundays in summer

C *Bramfield – Clibbons Post* About 1½ miles from the village, just beyond a dip in the lane past Bramfield Forest car park and on the left of the road is a post, placed there in 1927 by the East Herts. Archaeological Society. It marks the spot where local men dealt with William Clibbon, highwayman, in 1782. He was done to death and buried with a stake through his heart to prevent him doing further mischief

D *Aston Bury* Working farm open to visitors during the summer

E *Aston* View over the Beane Valley from along this lane, possibly one of the best views in the county

RIDE No 8

Easy Pedalling in East Herts

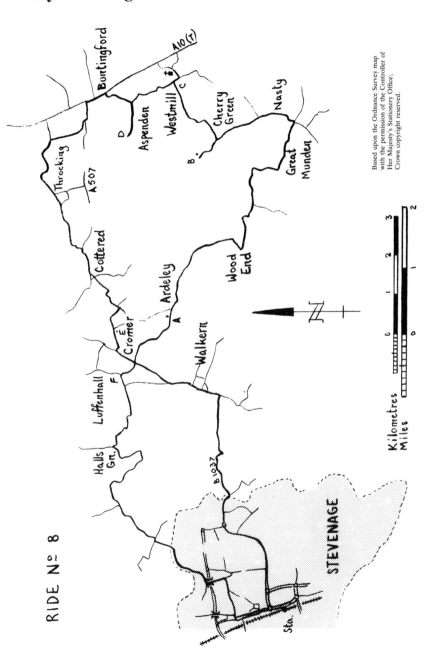

Based upon the Ordnance Survey map with the permission of the Controller of Her Majesty's Stationery Office; Crown copyright reserved.

RIDE Nº 8

Button Snap

Gentle pedalling through quiet villages with thatched cottages in surprising, hidden Hertfordshire. No spectacular views or breathtaking heights, but miles of pleasant lanes and peaceful cycling in some of the finest countryside within 30 miles of Central London. We encounter some of the most beautiful villages in the county and a cottage once owned by Charles Lamb, who wrote so kindly about Hertfordshire

Map: Sheet 166 in the O.S. Landranger series

Based on Stevenage – 28 miles (alternatively 13 miles)
Alternatively, using Ride No 2, from Baldock – add 18 miles; Letchworth – add 16 miles; or Hitchin – add 14 miles

1 Stevenage Station to Walkern
From STEVENAGE Station descend to the cycleway between the car park and the rail track. Turn right (northwards) and descend through the first underpass. At a T-junction turn right (signposted 'All areas except Gunnels Wood') and continue forward on the cycleway alongside Fairlands Way. Take care crossing Popple Way (*only interruption on 2 miles of cycleway*) and keep going until cycleway ends near a school. Join the road on the right (Walkern Road, B1037 and continue in the same direction until you reach WALKERN.

2 Walkern to Great Munden
At a T-junction, turn left (signposted B1037, Cottered). On entering CROMER village, turn right to ARDELEY (**A**). Go through this village and continue forward for 4½ miles via MOOR GREEN

and WOOD END to GREAT MUNDEN. Note the characteristic 'Hertfordshire spike' on top of Great Munden church tower.

3 Great Munden to Buntingford
At Great Munden turn left near the church and forward through NASTY, CHERRY GREEN (**B**), WESTMILL (**C**), and ASPENDEN (**D**) to BUNTINGFORD. Turn left into the village.

4 Buntingford to Cromer
In Buntingford High Street turn left (B1038 signposted Baldock, Cambridge) to the roundabout on the A10. Leave by the third exit to follow the A10 towards Royston for ½ mile, and then turn left to ride through a delightful lane to THROCKING. Straight on through the village to COTTERED. Join the A507 with care and in the middle of the village turn left on the B1037 to CROMER (**E**).

5 Cromer to Stevenage
Ride through Cromer and then take a right turn to LUFFENHALL (**F**). At the beginning of the village turn left (signposted Weston), go up a short hill and at the top keep forward to HALL'S GREEN. At the start of the village proper, ½ mile beyond the village sign and just before the Rising Sun PH, turn sharp left into a narrow, twisting lane to emerge at a corner with the Anchor PH on your

Westmill

33

right. Continue to STEVENAGE. On reaching a new estate road turn left for ¼ mile, then take a footpath on the right to lead through to the old road. At St Nicholas' Church, Stevenage, turn left into Almonds Lane and then right into Walkern Road. At the end, turn left in the High Street. Soon, where the street narrows, turn right into Drapers Way, to reach a cycleway beyond the lorry park on the left. Turn left on the cycleway alongside Lytton Way till you reach a T-junction and here turn right under Lytton Way. Turn left and after ¼ mile turn left again and immediately right to STEVENAGE Station.

Short cut to omit 15 miles – From Cromer to Stevenage
At CROMER in Section 2, turn left to LUFFENHALL to rejoin main ride at Section 5.

Points of Interest

A   Ardeley   A gem of a village – a collection of thatched cottages around a green, with a fine church and a pub

B   Cherry Green – Button Snap   At Cherry Green, where the lane bends right, if you make a detour ½ mile to the left you can see on the right the pretty thatched cottage which writer Charles Lamb owned from 1812 to 1815. Now owned by the Charles Lamb Society, this is not generally open to the public

C   Westmill   Beyond Cherry Green, at a T-junction at the foot of a gentle descent, detour slightly to the right to visit this village which is considered to be one of the prettiest villages in the county. Who would disagree?

D   Aspenden   Where the lane goes right, around the village green, the village is to the left. It is well worth a detour of ½ mile

E   Cromer mill   This 17th century post mill makes a landmark in this part of the county, standing, as it does, on a hill just before the descent into the village.

F   Luffenhall   Delightful collection of thatched and pargetted cottages

RIDE No 9

On the Borders of Essex

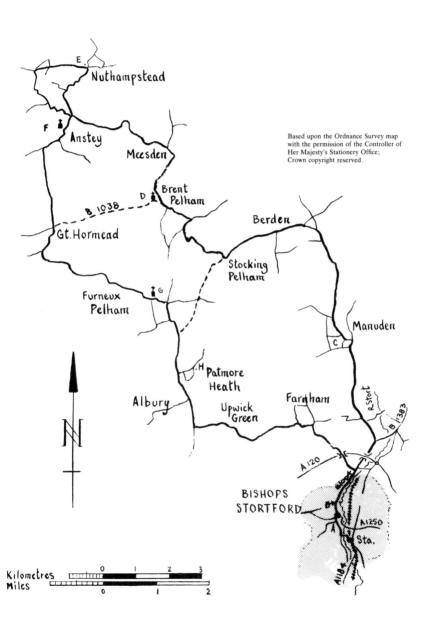

Based upon the Ordnance Survey map
with the permission of the Controller of
Her Majesty's Stationery Office;
Crown copyright reserved.

35

landscape near Manud...

Gently undulating, open country with many thatched cottages with timbered or pargetted walls. A few miles of Essex are included, but they are not distinguishable from this corner of Hertfordshire, which is characterised by its wide, open skylines. Discover a set of village stocks, a lock-up in a church gate, a moated Norman castle mound and a monument to airmen relating to World War 2

Maps: Sheets 167, 166 and 154 (little) in the O.S. Landranger series

Based on Bishop's Stortford – 30 miles (alternatively 27, 23 or 17 miles)

1 Bishop's Stortford to Manuden

Leave BISHOPS STORTFORD (**A**) Station yard and turn left into Station Road (one-way) and at the end turn right into Potter Street and then go straight on, along North Street, to the end. Turn right into Hadham Road to a roundabout on the B1004. Take the first exit, signposted Newport (**B**).

After a mile, where the B1004 bears right go straight on, and then, after another ½ mile, at another right hand bend, continue forward again for 2 miles to MANUDEN (**C**).

If the traffic is heavy, on leaving the Station yard it may be better to go straight on walking down Dane Street, a one-way street, to Hockerill Street. Turn left and then ride to the roundabout on the B1004. Take the 2nd exit to join the ride as described above.

2 Manuden to Brent Pelham

Beyond Manuden continue forward, with the River Stort in the valley on your right for 2½ miles. Soon after a turning to Little London, and opposite Highlands Farm, turn left to BERDEN and forward to STOCKING PELHAM. Turn right at the Cock PH and after one mile, turn left on the B1038 to BRENT PELHAM.

3 Brent Pelham to Great Hormead

At the church (**D**) continue forward, and taking care on a sharp right bend just past the Black Horse PH, continue straight on through MEESDEN to ANSTEY. On entering Anstey, turn right along a twisting lane to NUTHAMPSTEAD (**E**). At a junction just past the Woodman PH turn left (signposted Barkway) and descend gently through the village. At the foot of the descent turn left again (no signpost) to return via another twisting lane to ANSTEY, passing the village pump. Turn right through the village (**F**), and soon after the last houses turn left (signposted Flint Hall). To the right is the valley of the River Quin and you can see the radio mast at Coles Park, near Puckeridge. Continue on this lane for 2 miles to GREAT HORMEAD.

4 Great Hormead to Bishop's Stortford

Turn right onto the B1038, then immediately left by the Three Turns PH and after ½ mile turn left again to LITTLE HORMEAD and continue forward for 2 miles to FURNEUX PELHAM (**G**). Beyond the church turn right at the Brewery Tap PH, and soon left and then at a T-junction right again to ALBURY (**H**). Half a mile beyond the village, and just past a wood, turn left to UPWICK GREEN.

Continue straight on, and at two junctions near FARNHAM bear right towards BISHOP'S STORTFORD and continue forward to the B1004. Turn right into Rye Street; continue for a mile to a roundabout and take the first exit, The Causeway, which becomes Hockerill Street. After ¼ mile, turn right into Dane Street and back to the Station.

Short Cuts

1 To omit 13 miles – From Stocking Pelham to Furneux Pelham
At STOCKING PELHAM continue forward to FURNEUX PELHAM and ALBURY and rejoin the main ride in Section 4.

2 To omit 7 miles – From Brent Pelham to Great Hormead direct
At BRENT PELHAM turn left on the B1038 to GREAT HORMEAD, where turn left by the Three Tuns PH to rejoin the main ride at Section 4.

3 To omit 3 miles – Omission of Nuthampstead circuit
In Section 3, omit the circuit to Nuthampstead, and continue through
ANSTEY.

Points of Interest

A *Bishop's Stortford* Castle near Hockerill Street.
The Old Vicarage, in South Road is now the Rhodes Museum and
Commonwealth Centre. This birthplace of Cecil Rhodes is now a
private museum of his life and times.
Museum of local history, Apton Road.
Tourist Information Centre at 2, The Causeway

B *River Stort* To the right, the River Stort runs close by the road.
Near Stane Close on the right, and on the line of the Roman Stane
Street, was the ford from which the town name derives

C *Manuden* A splendid Essex village full of typical cottages

D *Brent Pelham* Stocks with five leg holes in front of the church

E *Nuthampstead* Near the Woodman PH there is a memorial to
US Air Force personnel who served at the nearby airfield in Scales
Park in World War 2

F *Anstey* Lockup in the church gate, in use until 1914. A moated
Norman castle mound lies behind the church

G *Furneux Pelham* Unusual inscription on the church tower –
'Time flies. Mind your business'.

H *Patmore Heath* To the left, before Albury is a nature reserve

RIDE No 10

Between the Stort and the Rib

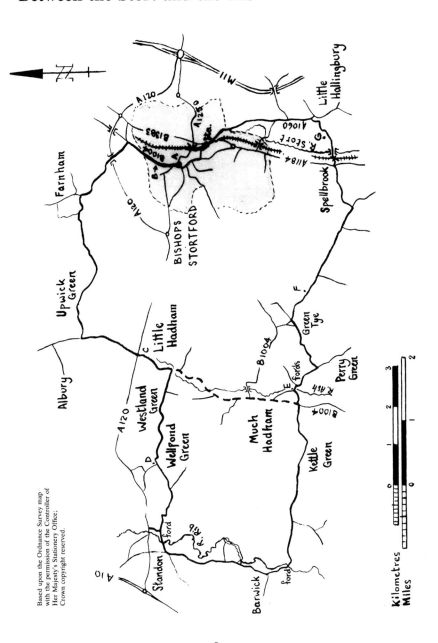

This ride is through quiet, gently undulating countryside which Charles Lamb, who spent some of his childhood nearby and often visited later, described as happy and homely. On your way you encounter many old cottages and houses, thatched, timbered or pargetted. In several places you will enjoy wide views so typical of this side of the county. You start and finish by the River Stort, and on the western side of the ride you cross the Rib twice, following its course for a few miles. In between you can see the delightful River Ash

Map: Sheets 166 and 167 in the O.S. Landranger series

Based on Bishop's Stortford – 23 miles (alternatively 16 miles)
Alternatively from Sawbridgeworth – an additional 5 miles

1 Bishop's Stortford to Little Hadham

On leaving BISHOP'S STORTFORD (**A**) Station yard, turn left into Station Road (one-way) and at the end turn right into Potter Street and then go straight on, along North Street to the end. Turn right into Hadham Road to a roundabout on the B1004.

Take the first exit (B1004) signposted Newport. After ¾ mile (**B**), turn left (signposted Farnham). After a further 1¼ miles, turn left (signposted Albury, Upwick) and soon left again to follow signs to Albury as far as a T-junction. Turn left to LITTLE HADHAM (**C**). Continue straight on at the traffic lights for ½ mile.

If traffic is heavy, on leaving the Station yard it may be better to go straight on walking down Dane Street, a one-way street, to Hocker-ill Street. Turn left here and forward to the roundabout, where you take the 2nd exit to join the main ride as described above.

2 Little Hadham to Hadham Cross

Near the Nag's Head PH turn right to WESTLAND GREEN. If the hill out of Little Hadham causes you to walk, enjoy the view over your shoulder. Continue forward to WELLPOND GREEN (**D**) and to STANDON. (*Ignore the Standon sign at Wellpond Green: it directs via A120.*) At Standon, detour through the High Street but leave by Paper Mill Lane, which is to the left as you enter the village (signposted 'Ford. Unsuitable for motors'). Note the old rail crossing shortly before crossing the bridged ford and then on to a T-junction, here turn left. Follow the delightful lane for 2½ miles to BARWICK, but take care on the bends. Cars are few but they seem to pop up quickly. At Barwick bear left via a bridged ford and then uphill through Sawtrees Wood and forward to HADHAM CROSS.

3 Hadham Cross to Little Hallingbury

At the B1004 turn left and immediately right by the Old Crown PH. Soon bear right to cross the River Ash and forward (**E**) to a T-

Much Hadham

junction, where turn right by Sidehill House. At the top of the hill
(PERRY GREEN) turn left by the church and through GREEN
TYE to an offset crossroads, where turn right (signposted
Spellbrook). Continue forward for 2 miles (**F**), and then soon after
TRIMS GREEN turn left to SPELLBROOK. At the A1184 turn
left and immediately right (Spellbrook Lane East) to cross the River
Stort and River Stort navigation (**G**) to the A1060 (the George Inn).

4   Little Hallingbury to Bishops Stortford
At the A1060 turn left for 2 miles to BISHOP'S STORTFORD. At
a roundabout continue forward (signposted Town Centre) to some
traffic lights, where a left turn into Hockerill Street and soon another
left turn into Dane Street brings you to the station.

Note: The A120 road is **NOT** recommended as a short cut from Little
Hadham on this ride. It is narrow and carries much fast and heavy
traffic.

Short cut to omit 7 miles – From Hadham Ford to Hadham Cross
At LITTLE HADHAM (end of Section 1) continue straight on and
through MUCH HADHAM to the crossroads near the Old Crown
PH. Turn left and read from Section 3.

Alternative start and finish at Sawbridgeworth

Start
Leave SAWBRIDGEWORTH Station yard and turn left over the
level crossing. Soon turn left again (signposted Little Hallingbury).
Continue forward for 2 miles through GASTON GREEN to the

A1060, where turn left. After ½ mile, at the George Inn, continue forward to join the main ride at Section 4.

Finish
At the George Inn at the end of Section 3, turn right on the A1060 for ½ mile, and then turn right again (signposted Gaston Green) and continue for 2 miles to a T-junction. SAWBRIDGEWORTH Station is 200 yards to the right.

Points of Interest

A   Bishop's Stortford   Local history museum in Apton Road. The Old Vicarage, South Street, is now the Rhodes Museum and Commonwealth Centre. This is a private museum of the life and times of Cecil Rhodes, who was born at the old vicarage. Tourist Information Centre at 2, The Causeway.
Castle near Hockerill Street

B   River Stort   To the right of the road is the River Stort. Near Stane Close on the right, and on the line of the Roman Stane Street, was the ford from which the town takes its name

C   Little Hadham   As you wait at the traffic lights, note the dates on the nearby houses – 1726, 1500 and 1672. Beyond the crossroads are more old cottages

D   From The Nags Head PH, Wellpond Green   a detour can be made via Braughing, returning to Standon. Turn right opposite the PH and follow Sections 3 and 4 of Ride No 11, rejoining this ride at Standon in Section 2

E   Much Hadham   After heavy rain the stretch of road beyond the ford may be flooded. You may then prefer to detour through Much Hadham High Street and turn right on the B1004 towards Bishops Stortford for 1½ miles. Then turn right (signposted Green Tye) to a crossroads, where keep straight on towards Spellbrook

F   Remains of a wartime airfield   On the left of the road just beyond the crossroads is a brick and concrete gun emplacement built in World War 2 when a German invasion was a strong possibility. Remains of airfield roads can also be seen

G   Spellbrook – Wallbury   Site of Iron Age settlement *c* 300BC. Earthworks can be seen in the private woods close to the road on the left at the top of a short hill beyond the rivers

42

RIDE No 11

Hidden Villages of East Herts

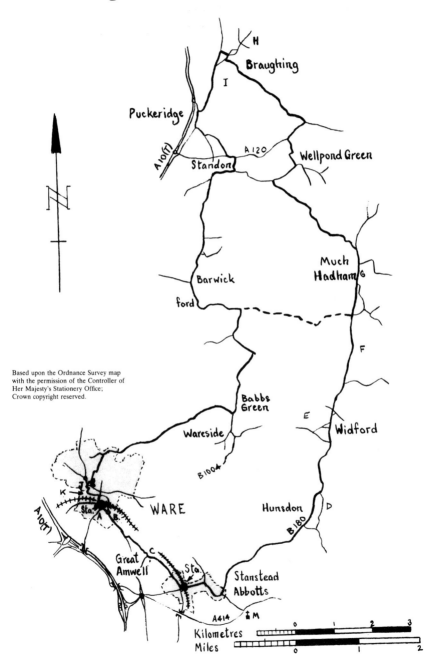

Based upon the Ordnance Survey map
with the permission of the Controller of
Her Majesty's Stationery Office;
Crown copyright reserved.

This ride is based on the town of Ware, famous for its malting industry, its Great Bed and as the terminus of John Gilpin's ride in the poem by William Cowper. It includes a mixture of open countryside, wooded lanes and villages with old buildings and secret corners – typical Hertfordshire. Some of the villages on this ride were featured in a programme by Anglia Television some years ago. A team of television producers got lost between London and Norwich, missing the A11 road. They could hardly believe their eyes, and so returned to make a film 'The hidden villages of Hertfordshire'

Map: Sheet 166 in the O.S. Landranger series

Based on Ware – 27 miles (alternatively – 16 miles)
Alternatively from Hoddesdon (Rye House) – 31 or 20 miles

1   Ware to St Margarets
From WARE Station turn left and then left again over the level crossing (**A**) and again left into London Road (**B**). After ½ mile, at a roundabout take the second exit and follow the A1170 for ½ mile. Near the foot of Amwell Hill turn left over a new river bridge and along Lower Road to GREAT AMWELL (**C**). Continue forward to ST MARGARETS.

2   St Margarets to Much Hadham
Turn left and over the level crossing to STANSTEAD ABBOTTS. At the end of the High Street bear right and at the foot of a hill bear left to follow the B180 to HUNSDON (**D**) and WIDFORD (**E**). Turn right on the B1004 to MUCH HADHAM (**F**) and (**G**).

3   Much Hadham to Braughing
About ¼ mile beyond the village, turn left (signposted Standon, Wellpond Green) and continue forward for 2 miles. On some high ground with extensive views, turn sharp right to WELLPOND GREEN. Opposite the Nag's Head PH turn left (signposted Standon), then right and left to reach the A120. Turn right on the A120 with care and soon left to BRAUGHING (**H**). Take care also on the final descent to the village, which ends at a T-junction, where we turn right to the village proper.

4   Braughing to Barwick
Leave Braughing towards Puckeridge and soon join the B1368 (**I**) to PUCKERIDGE, to turn left near the White Hart PH, just before a large roundabout, into the High Street. In the High Street turn left into Station Road and continue forward to STANDON. At the A120 turn left (*with care because of heavy traffic*), over the river and immediately right into the High Street. At the end of the High

Amwell Nature Reserve

Street, just past the church, turn right by a piece of puddingstone set on a flint plinth, to leave Standon via Paper Mill Lane. Cross a bridged ford and at a T-junction, turn left. Take care on the many bends in this delightful lane for 2½ miles to BARWICK.

5   Barwick to Ware

Bear left and soon cross another bridged ford. Continue forward to the top of the hill and to a turning right (signposted Thundridge). Here turn right and soon left (signposted Babbs Green) to descend gently for 2 miles to BABBS GREEN, where turn right and on past Noah's Ark farm and Fanhams Hall to WARE. Enter Ware via Fanhams Hall Road which becomes High Oak Road, (*take care on the descent*).

At the bottom turn right into Collett Road and soon left into Crib Street. At the end turn right into Church Street to enter High Street next to St Mary's Church (**J**). Cross the High Street opposite the church and through the car park next to the Brewery Tap PH to cross the River Lea by a footbridge. Turn left on the tow path (**K**) to Amwell End where turn right to Ware Station.

Short cut to omit 11 miles – From Hadham Cross to near Barwick
In Section 2, at Hadham Cross (crossroads near the Old Crown PH
on the right) turn left (no signpost) and through KETTLE GREEN
to a turning to the left (signposted Babbs Green, Wareside). Here
turn left and rejoin the main ride in Section 5.

Alternative start and finish at Rye House Station, Hoddesdon

Start
On leaving RYE HOUSE Station turn right into Rye Road (**L**) and
forward for 1½ miles along a toll road to a T-junction with the B181
(**M**). Turn left towards Stanstead Abbotts for ½ mile. Just before a
steep descent turn right to join B180 and then right again towards
HUNSDON to join main ride in Section 2.

Finish
At ST MARGARETS (end of Section 1) turn right and immediately
left (signposted Rye Park). After a mile turn left into Old Highway
to its end, where turn left again into Rye Road to RYE HOUSE
Station.

Points of Interest

A   Amwell House   Building opposite Amwell End. Home in 18th
century of Quaker poet John Scott. In recent times used as Ware
Grammar School and now Ware College. In Scotts Road (a short
distance to the right) in a private garden but open to the public
occasionally, is an underground grotto constructed by Scott

B   New River   On our left for 1 mile is this aqueduct constructed
between 1608 and 1613 on the initiative of Sir Hugh Myddleton, an
Alderman of the City of London, who initially financed the project
at his own expense. The objective was to supply London with fresh
water from the springs at Chadwell, (½ mile to the right towards
Hertford). The supply was later supplemented from the River Lea
and boreholes along its route. Pumping stations can be seen at
Amwell Hill and between Great Amwell and St Margarets

C   Great Amwell   On an island in the New River is a memorial to Sir
Hugh Myddleton. Opposite this and down a few steps is 'Emma's Well'
from which the village takes it name. Emma is thought by some
historians to have been the wife of Ethelred the Dane. On his death she
married Canute

46

D Hunsdon Little remains now of the airfield to the right, used in World War 2. Mosquito bombers flew from here to precision-bomb the jail in Amiens (France) enabling resistance fighters to escape

E Widford – Blakesware Manor A mile to the left (not open to public). The maternal grandmother of writer Charles Lamb, Mrs Mary Field was housekeeper at the former Blakesware Manor for over 50 years, and is buried in Widford churchyard. Lamb often visited Blakesware in his youth and in his later years

F Much Hadham – Ginger Cress Farm On the right at the top of a gentle rise ¼ mile past 'Much Hadham' sign. Trout farm and wetlands interpretive centre. Farm walk and nature trail

G Much Hadham main street Fine collection of jettied, half-timbered and pargetted houses. A farmhouse near the church was for 800 years the country Palace of the Bishops of London. Here in 1430 was born to the widow of Henry V, Edmund Tudor, father of Henry VII

H Braughing The village is to the right at a T-junction. Exceptionally unspoilt village with two fords. Worth spending a while exploring. On summer Sunday afternoons teas are served in a fine building opposite the church

I Site of Roman town (Just before the bridge over the River Rib, to the right). The site is not open to public. To the left, in Gatesbury Wood is an ancient earthwork

J Ware Priory Opposite St Mary's Church and set back from the road, this 14th century Franciscan Friary is now used as Council offices

K Ware, gazebos by the River Lea Unique wooden summer houses. Note the sweet smell from the maltings, for which the town was famous. As the towpath ends by the bridge, to the left is the Saracen's Head Inn, recently rebuilt. An inn of this name on this site was the original home of the Great Bed of Ware, referred to by Shakespeare in *Twelfth Night*, and now in the Victoria and Albert Museum

L Rye House Only the 15th century gatehouse remains of the house where in 1683 a plot was hatched to murder Charles II

M Stanstead Abbots A short detour to the right towards Roydon will bring you to the church of St James. No longer regularly used for worship, but maintained by the Redundant Churches Fund, this church has an unusual three-tiered pulpit

RIDE No 12

The Rib Valley

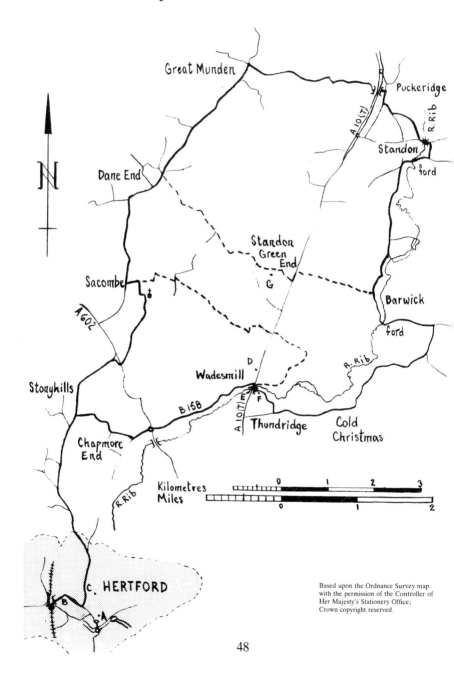

Based upon the Ordnance Survey map
with the permission of the Controller of
Her Majesty's Stationery Office;
Crown copyright reserved.

48

This ride follows the course of the River Rib, starting from Hertford, where, together with the Beane and the Mimram it joins the River Lea. We travel through some open country with fine views such as that near Sawtrees Farm, adjacent to the quaintly-named hamlet of Cold Christmas. We cross two fords, (bridged for the cautious rider), and return through quiet countryside.

This ride and its short cuts cross the A10. This is usually a busy road and is not recommended for riding. Cross it with care

Map: Sheet 166 in the O.S. Landranger series

Based on Hertford – 25 miles (alternatively 21 or 15 miles)

1 Hertford to Wadesmill

From HERTFORD NORTH Station (**A**) cross the road to Beane Road (**B**). Follow Beane Road and at its end turn right into Molewood Road. At the end use the footpath ahead through to Port Vale. At the end turn left into Port Hill (B158), a steep ascent (**C**). Beyond the top of the hill at a mini roundabout take the second exit into Sacombe Road for 2 miles to STONYHILLS. By the Three Harts PH turn right (no sign) to CHAPMORE END. At the pond turn left to descend to the B158, where turn left and continue straight on to WADESMILL (**D and E**).

2 Wadesmill to Standon

Cross the A10 and turn right over the river bridge. Immediately turn left and continue along Old Church Lane, by the river. After ½ mile (**F**) bear right to climb a narrow lane and at the top turn left and continue through COLD CHRISTMAS. Carry straight on and a mile beyond Sawtrees Farm, at a T-junction, turn left to descend to BARWICK FORD. Cross the bridged ford and bear right for ½ mile to BARWICK. Turn right to follow a narrow lane for 2½ miles to STANDON. (*Take care on the many bends. The few cars on this lane appear to come up quickly.*)

At a right junction, with a small island, just before reaching the A120, turn right (signposted 'Ford. Unsuitable for motors'). Recross the River Rib via a bridged ford to enter the village at the end of the High Street. Turn sharp left into the High Street.

3 Standon to Sacombe

At the far end turn left with care onto the A120, cross the river bridge and immediately turn right at The Heron PH along Station Road to PUCKERIDGE, turning right into the High Street. Leave

Hertford Castle

Puckeridge via Mentley Lane East (on the left side of the High Street). Use the overgrown footpath on the left at the end to reach the A10. Cross the dual carriageway with care and continue forward in Mentley Lane West to GREAT MUNDEN. Here turn left and follow through for 4 miles via DANE END to SACOMBE.

4 Sacombe to Hertford

Turn left in the village (signposted Sacombe Green End) and soon turn right to the church. Beyond the church keep straight on the bridleway. This is stony for a short distance, but rideable, and soon follows the line of a surfaced driveway to the A602. Cross this road and turn half right to follow the lane for 3 miles, through STONYHILLS to join the B158 at a mini roundabout in BENGEO.

Taking the second exit continue for ½ mile to descend Port Hill with care. At the bottom turn right into Port Vale, and at the end continue on the footpath to Molewood Road. Soon turn left into Beane Road to the station.

Short Cuts

1 To omit 4 miles – from Barwick to Dane End
At BARWICK (Section 2), turn left to the A10. Turn left onto the A10 and immediately right, by the Happy Eater restaurant, through

50

STANDON GREEN END (G) to DANE END to rejoin the main ride in Section 3.

2 To omit 10 miles – From Wadesmill to Sacombe

At WADESMILL (Section 1) turn left and cross the A10 by the Feathers Inn to take Youngsbury Lane. Soon, at the end continue on a bridleway. This is rough for a few yards, but then runs along the drive. Climb gently towards Youngsbury House, to bear left by a mews building, and then to enter HIGH CROSS via North Drive. At the end turn left and immediately right into Marshalls Lane to SACOMBE GREEN, where continue forward to descend to SACOMBE. On the descent to the village, turn left to the church to rejoin the main ride at Section 4.

Points of Interest

A Hertford Site of Synod of Bishops 673 AD – details of this event can be found on a tablet in the grounds of the 16th Century Castle, now used as offices for the Town and District Councils, and a tourist information centre. Museum in Bull Plain includes the Hertfordshire Regiment museum

B Hertford To the right is the course of the railway that once linked Hertford North and East Stations. Near McMullen's brewery is the site of the original Hertford Station opened in the 1850s, closed in the 1920s and demolished in 1992.

C Bengeo St Leonard's, a little Norman church with 13th century wall paintings is about ½ mile off to the right of the ride

D Wadesmill – Clarkson monument At the side of the A10 road, a little way up the hill to the left, is a monument to Thomas Clarkson. It marks the spot where he picnicked with friends on a ride from Cambridge, and resolved to take steps to abolish slavery

E Wadesmill – bridge Built in 1825 by the Cheshunt Turnpike Trust; when viewed from the riverside, the pleasing style of the structure can be appreciated

F Thundridge Where the lane turns right, a short way along the track ahead is the ruin of Thundridge Old Church

G Standon Green End A stone records the landing of the first successful aerial flight in 1784 from Moorfields in London by the Italian balloonist Vincenza Lunardi. The stone is in a field behind 'Great Mead' on the left of the lane, about ¼ mile from the A10.

RIDE No 13

Secrets of South East Herts

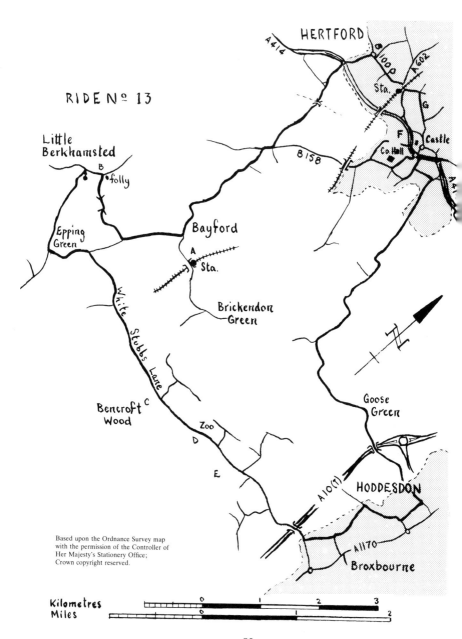

RIDE Nº 13

Little Berkhamsted

B
folly

Epping Green

Bayford

A
Sta.

Brickendon Green

White Stubbs Lane

Bencroft Wood
C

Zoo
D

E

Goose Green

HERTFORD

A414

A1000

A602

Sta.

G

F
Castle

Co. Hall

B158

A10

A10(T)

HODDESDON

A1170

Broxbourne

Kilometres
Miles

0 1 2 3

0 1 2

In the angle between the A10 and A414 roads lies this fascinating circuit. Untouched and unseen by the streams of traffic on these trunk roads, it is a mixture of wooded lanes and high, open ground affording splendid views which are a little surprising since one is hardly aware of having climbed any hills. Those riders who fancy something a little more hilly can ride a little farther south by linking this ride with Number 14.

Woodland walks and a wildlife park are encountered on this circuit and we suggest a quiet way through Hertford which includes a riverside pub and a station closed 30 years before Dr Beeching swung his axe

Map: Sheet 166 in the O.S. Landranger series

Based on Hertford – 18 miles
Alternatively from Broxbourne – 18 miles; Hoddesdon (Rye House) – 19 miles; or Cheshunt – 24 miles

1 Hertford to Bayford
From HERTFORD NORTH Station turn left into North Road (A119), and almost immediately left again (signposted Welwyn, B1001). Climb the hill and continue for ½ mile to a roundabout and then take the first exit to descend to HERTINGFORDBURY. Cross the A414 and enter the village. Opposite the White Horse Inn turn left in St Mary's Lane and continue forward for 1 mile to the B158. Turn right and soon left to BAYFORD.

2 Bayford to Broxbourne
In the village (**A**) bear right at The Baker Arms PH towards Epping Green and after ¾ mile, where the lane bends left, turn right in Bucks Alley, which is unsignposted. A steep descent is followed by a climb to LITTLE BERKHAMSTED (**B**). At the end of Bucks Alley, turn left and at Little Berkhamsted Church turn left again to EPPING GREEN. Beyond the village turn left towards Bayford and continue forward in White Stubbs Lane for 4 miles, past Bencroft Wood (**C**) (**D**) (**E**) to enter BROXBOURNE via Baas Hill. Soon after crossing the A10 road-bridge take the second turn left, (Baas Lane) and at the end turn left into Park Lane and bear right.

3 Broxbourne to Hertford
At the end of Park Lane turn right into Cock Lane for ½ mile, and beyond a childrens playground turn left into Park View, which becomes Rose Vale. At the end turn left into Lord Street. Continue forward for 5 miles to HERTFORD.

Enter Hertford via Mangrove Road. Just past Simon Balle School on the right, and in sight of a main road, turn *SHARP* left into Hagsdell Road to the end. Turn right into Queens Road. At the bottom of the hill use the subway to cross the ring road and emerge in Fore Street opposite Shire Hall.

Hertford, St Andrews Street

4A   Through Hertford

The most direct route to Hertford North Station is as follows, but it could be busy. See Section 4B for a slightly longer but quieter route.

Turn left in Fore Street (walking the one-way system), to Parliament Square (the War Memorial). Turn right into The Wash to pass the entrance to the Castle (**F**) and cross Mill Bridge. At Old Cross continue forward in St Andrews Street which becomes North Road and leads to the station.

4B   Alternative quieter route through Hertford

Cross Fore Street and go round Shire Hall to Salisbury Square. Go forward and half left into Bull Plain (where the museum is situated). At the end cross the narrow bridge and continue forward via The Folly. Turn left into Thornton Street and then cross the footbridge to Hartham Lane (**G**). At the end turn right into Cowbridge and bear left off the main road into Port Vale. At the end use the footpath through to Molewood Road, and then turn left into Beane Road to the station.

Alternative Starts and Finishes

1   Broxbourne

Start

Leave BROXBOURNE Station yard and turn right into Station

Road. At the end turn left into High Road (A1170) and immediately turn right into Park Lane. Join the main ride at Section 3.

To omit Hertford
In Section 3, when reaching Queens Road turn left and at the top of the hill turn right into Highfield Road. At the end turn left into Bullocks Lane to descend steeply. At the bottom turn left to follow the B158 for 1½ miles. Turn left to BAYFORD, and join the main ride from Section 2.

Finish
At Park Lane (end of Section 2) turn right into High Road (A1170), where turn left and immediately right into Station Road to the station.

2   Hoddesdon (Rye House)
Start
Leave RYE HOUSE Station and turn left into Rye Road. At the end, at a double roundabout, turn right and left into Middlefield Road. At the end turn left into Ware Road (A1170) and soon at a roundabout take the third exit (Hertford Road). (*Take care as this short stretch can be busy, although there is a footpath.*) Soon turn left into Norris Lane and right into Winterscroft Road. Continue forward to the end, and then turn right into Lord Street to join the main ride at Section 3.

To omit Hertford
See note under alternative start and finish for Broxbourne

Finish
At Section 3, on entering Lord Street, immediately turn right into Langton Road. At the end turn right into Winterscroft Road, then left into Norris Lane and then right into Hertford Road to descend to a roundabout. Turn left into Ware Road (A1170) and soon right into Middlefield Road. (*Care on this busy stretch.*) At the end (at a double roundabout) turn right and left into Rye Road to the station.

3   Cheshunt
Start
Leave CHESHUNT Station and turn left into Windmill Lane to the end. Turn right into Turners Hill for ½mile and then left into Church Lane. Cross the A10 at some traffic lights and continue forward to a roundabout by the Jolly Bricklayers PH. Take the third exit (Flamstead End Road). Soon at a second roundabout continue forward (signposted Newgatestreet) and soon turn right into Park Lane. Continue forward into Park Lane Paradise, and then descend Holy Cross Hill (**H**). At the bottom turn left into West End Road to

WORMLEY WEST END. Soon, just past the Woodman PH, turn right to a T-junction. Here turn right into White Stubbs Lane to join main ride in Section 2.

To omit Hertford
See note under Broxbourne above

Finish
In White Stubbs Lane, soon after Bencroft Wood car park, turn right to Wormley West End. Beyond the village turn right to climb Holy Cross Hill. Continue forward into Park Lane Paradise, and Park Lane. Soon after the speed limit signs, at a T-junction, turn left into Longfield Lane. Soon, at a roundabout, take the second exit (B156), and at a second roundabout by the Jolly Bricklayers PH, take the first exit into Church Lane. Cross the A10 at traffic lights, and at the end turn right into Turners Hill. After ½ mile, turn left into Windmill Lane to the station.

Points of Interest

A *Bayford Station* It is worth a detour of ¼ mile towards Brickendon to see this small country station which appears to have escaped from a model railway

B *Little Berkhamsted – Stratton's Folly* This tower – on your right as you approach Little Berkhamsted is said to have been built so its owner could see his ships coming up the Thames!

C *Bencroft Wood* Short woodland trail

D *Paradise Wildlife Park – White Stubbs Lane* Large area including animal park, woodland railway, children's play area and refreshments

E *Occasional views* through trees on the right over the Lea Valley to high ground in Essex

F *Hertford* See general note under Ride No 12

G *Hertford* To the right is the course of a railway which once linked Hertford East and North Stations. A short way along it, to the rear of McMullen's brewery is the site of the 1850s station, closed once the North Station was built in the 1920s, and demolished in 1992.

H *Holy Cross Hill* At the foot of the hill on the right, is a London Coal Duty Boundary marker, one of a series across south Hertfordshire, indicating the boundary within which the City Corporation could levy a duty on coal and wine brought in. The duty, originally imposed in 1667 to help rebuild the City after the great fire, was abolished in 1889

RIDE No 14

Surprising South Hertfordshire

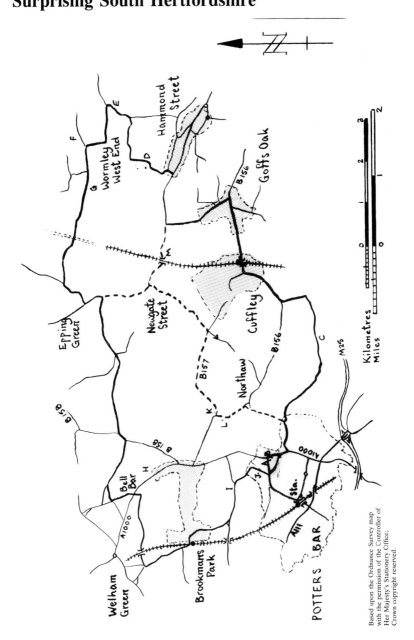

Based upon the Ordnance Survey map
with the permission of the Controller of
Her Majesty's Stationery Office;
Crown copyright reserved.

57

A surprising, hilly and wooded piece of countryside is sandwiched between the M25, A1(M), A414 and the A10, four traffic arteries whose users probably have no idea of what a pleasant area lies so close to their speeding routes. Take time and enjoy one of the best parts of Hertfordshire, even though it borders Greater London. Perhaps the sudden transition from town to country is the biggest surprise of all.

Watch out for a relic of World War 2, and for some reminders of the Great Fire of London in 1666. Since the early part of this circuit is hilly a number of short cuts are suggested

Map: Sheet 166 in the O.S. Landranger series

Based on Potters Bar – 22 miles (alternatively 18, 17 or 12 miles) Alternatively from Cuffley or Brookmans Park – 21 or 16 miles; from Broxbourne – 26, 21, or 14 miles; or Cheshunt – 29, 24, or 17 miles

1   Potters Bar to Cuffley
Leave POTTERS BAR Station and turn left into Darkes Lane, which becomes Church Road. Keep straight on to the end (**A**). At Hatfield Road turn right (**B**) and soon, at some traffic lights, turn left into the B156 (The Causeway) for ½ mile. Near The Chequers PH turn right into Coopers Lane Road. Continue forward for 2 miles, past the GRA kennels (**C**). At the end turn left into Cattlegate Hill to descend to a T-junction with Northaw Road. Turn right to CUFFLEY. At a junction turn right (*care on double junction*) into Station Road (B156).

2   Cuffley to Wormley West End
Continue forward up Cuffley Hill to GOFFS OAK at the top. Turn left by the War Memorial (Newgate Street Road) for 1½ miles to the end. At a T-junction turn right into Hammond Street Road for a mile. As the road starts to descend turn left (*watch for oil on road by a bus turn-round*), into Smiths Lane and left again into Bread and Cheese Lane. Take care through this narrow, hilly stretch (**D**). At the end turn sharp right into Beaumont Road. Continue forward for ½ mile to a T-junction. Turn left to descend Holy Cross Hill (**E**) and at the bottom turn left into West End Road to WORMLEY WEST END.

3   Wormley West End to Bell Bar
Just past The Woodman PH turn right to a T-junction with White Stubbs Lane. Turn left into White Stubbs Lane (**F and G**) and forward for 3 miles to near EPPING GREEN. At a T-junction turn left towards Newgate Street. Descend for ¼ mile and then turn right to TYLERS CAUSEWAY and forward for 2 miles to a T-junction

with the B158. Turn left on the B158 and soon right (signposted Welham Green) to descend gently. At a crossroads at the bottom turn left (no signpost) to the A1000 at BELL BAR (**H**).

4   Bell Bar to Potters Bar

Cross the A1000 and forward in Bell Bar Lane. Soon turn right into Bulls Lane to WELHAM GREEN. After the rail bridge, at a T-junction, turn left to BROOKMANS PARK. Beyond the rail bridge at the station continue forward for 2 miles on Blue Bridge Road which becomes Hawkshead Road (**I**). Soon after entering the Potters Bar built-up area and before the A1000, turn right into Osborne Road (**J**) to a T-junction. Here turn right into Church Road, which becomes Darkes Lane and on to reach the station in ½ mile.

Short Cuts

1   To omit 4 miles – from near Epping Green via Newgate Street to Potters Bar
In Section 3, instead of turning right to Tylers Causeway, continue downhill and then climb to NEWGATE STREET. In the village, turn right towards Northaw. Descend a steep hill and climb to the B157, The Ridgeway. Here turn right towards Hatfield for 1½ miles. Where the road turns sharp right (**K**), turn left towards NORTHAW (**L**). At a T-junction with the B156 turn right to POTTERS BAR. At the traffic lights on the A1000 turn right and soon left into Billy Low's Lane. At the end turn left into Darkes Lane to the station.

Zeppelin memorial, Cuffley

2 To omit 10 miles – from Goffs Oak via Newgate Street to Potters Bar
At the end of Newgate Street Road (Section 2) turn left to NEW-GATE STREET (*steep descent* (**M**) *and climb*). Opposite the church turn left towards Northaw. Follow Short Cut 1 to Potters Bar.

3 To omit 5 miles – from Goffs Oak to Tylers Causeway
Proceed to NEWGATE STREET as described in Short Cut 2, but at the church continue forward for nearly a mile and then turn left to TYLERS CAUSEWAY to rejoin the main ride in Section 3.

Alternative starts and finishes

1 From Cuffey 21 or 16 miles (*or less using short cuts as above*)
Leave CUFFLEY Station yard and turn left into Station Road to join the main ride at Section 2.

To omit Potters Bar from main ride
In Section 4, at the end of Osborne Road, turn left into Church Road to join the main ride in Section 1.

To omit Potters Bar from Short Cut 1 – 16 miles
Half a mile after the right turn onto the B156, just past the Chequers PH, turn left into Coopers Lane Road to join the main ride in Section 1.

2 From Brookmans Park
Leave BROOKMAN'S PARK Station car park and turn right into Bradmore Green (Blue Bridge Road) to join main ride in Section 4.

To omit Potters Bar – see note above under Cuffley

3 From Broxbourne (26, 21 or 14 miles)
Start
Leave BROXBOURNE Station yard and turn right into Station Road. At the end turn left into High Road and immediately right into Park Lane. Soon, where Park Lane bears right, turn left into Baas Lane. Soon, at the end, turn right to cross the A10 road-bridge. Continue forward in Baas Hill, which becomes White Stubbs Lane. Join the main ride in Section 3 soon after Paradise Park (**F**).

To omit Potters Bar – see note above under Cuffley

Finish
At the junction with White Stubbs Lane in Section 3, turn right to descend Baas Hill. Soon after crossing A10 road-bridge, take the

second left (Baas Lane). At the end turn right into Park Lane and soon at the end, turn left into High Road. Soon again, turn right into Station Road to the station.

To omit 12 miles
At the turn to Tylers Causeway in Section 3, continue forward to Newgate Street and then forward via Darnicle Hill (*steep descent* (**M**) *and climb*) to Hammond Street. Rejoin the main ride at the end of Newgate Street Road in Section 2.

To omit 5 miles
At Tylers Causeway, follow Short Cut 1 via Newgate Street as far as the edge of Potters Bar on the B156. Turn left opposite the Chequers PH into Coopers Lane Road and join the main ride from Section 1 as far as White Stubbs Lane in Section 3.

4 From Cheshunt (29, 24 or 17 miles)
Start
Leave CHESHUNT Station and turn left into Windmill Lane to the end. Turn right into Turners Hill for ½ mile. Turn left into Church Lane, cross the A10 at the traffic lights. At a roundabout by the Jolly Bricklayers PH take the third exit (B156), Flamstead End Road. Soon, at a second roundabout continue forward (signposted Newgatestreet) and soo turn right into Park Lane. Continue forward in Park Lane Paradise, and then descend Holy Cross Hill (**E**) to join the main ride near the end of Section 2.

To omit Potters Bar – see note under Cuffley (above)

To omit either 12 or 5 miles – see notes under Broxbourne above

Finish
At the end of Beaumont Road in Section 2, turn right into Park Lane Paradise, which becomes Park Lane. Soon after the speed limit signs, at a T-junction turn left into Longfield Lane. Soon, at a roundabout, take the second exit (B156) and at the next roundabout, by the Jolly Bricklayers PH, take the first exit – Church Lane. Cross the A10 at the traffic lights and continue to the end. Turn right into Turners Hill for ½ mile, and then left into Windmill Lane to the station.

Points of Interest

A Potters Bar – Church Road On the right, 50 yards from the Hatfield Road is a London Coal Duty Boundary marker post, one of a series across the south of the county. They indicate the area within which the Corporation of the City of London was able to levy a duty on coal and wine. The duty was originally imposed by Act of Parliament in 1667 to help rebuild the City of London after the Great Fire. It was abolished in 1889 and these posts date from 1851

B *Potters Bar – Hatfield Road* On the right, 50 yards south of Church Road, another Coal Post.

C *Coopers Lane Road* Extensive views to right, somewhat spoiled by the M25, but at least that road has taken some of the traffic away from this ride

D *Bread and Cheese Lane* Notice an octagonal brick and concrete gun emplacement on the left. Built in the first year of World War 2 in case of enemy invasion, some are now preserved as buildings of historical interest

E *Holy Cross Hill* Near the bottom, on the right is another London Coal Duty Boundary marker

F *Paradise Wildlife Park – White Stubbs Lane* Large area including animal park, woodland railway, children's play area and refreshments. A short detour to the right

G *Bencroft Wood* Short woodland trail

H *Brookmans Park* To the left can be seen the radio transmission masts of the BBC station, established in 1929

I *Potters Bar – Hawkshead Road, The Folly* On the left, by the junction with Swanley Bar Lane is a Tudor brick arch. This was once the gateway to Gobions, the one-time home of Sir Thomas More, Lord Chancellor of England and the author of *Utopia*. Gobions was demolished in the 18th century and the park was incorporated into Brookmans, this house being destroyed by fire in 1891, leaving the arch in splendid loneliness

J *Potters Bar – Heath Road* Yet another Coal Post. A turning to the right off Osborne Road, about 100 yards down

K *The Ridgeway – near Cuffley* At the end, on the right in the hedge is another Coal Post

L *Northaw – Well Road* Near the entrance to Queenswood School is another Coal Post

M *Darnicle Lane – near Newgate Street* At the foot of the hill by the bridge, a Coal Post

RIDE No 15

Mid-Herts – Away from the A1(M)

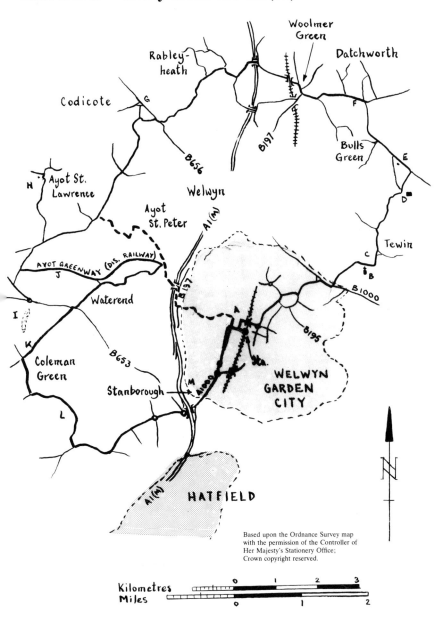

Based upon the Ordnance Survey map
with the permission of the Controller of
Her Majesty's Stationery Office;
Crown copyright reserved.

63

Tewin Church

On this ride, never farther than 3 miles from the A1(M), but rarely aware of its existence, we see ancient houses, a highwayman's resting place and a whipping post. We pass through a pre-Domesday village and ride a former railway track. With any luck we may also see one of the latest, relatively quiet aircraft fly over. And we have the mix of wooded lanes and open views which characterises Hertfordshire

Map: Sheet 166 in the O.S. Landranger series

Based on Welwyn Garden City – 23 miles (alternatively – 16 miles)
Alternatively from Hatfield – 26 miles

1 Welwyn Garden City to Tewin

From the front of WELWYN GARDEN CITY Station (**A**) turn right into Stonehills to a roundabout and then take the third exit – Bridge Road (B195). Cross the rail bridge to a roundabout and take the first exit into Bessemer Road. After ½ mile, at a one-way system (Mundells), take the second exit (Waterside). (*It may be better to use the cycleway on the left just before the roundabout. A somewhat complicated but well signed route leads to Waterside.*) Descend Waterside to a T-junction and turn right onto the B1000 towards Hertford and then soon turn left to TEWIN (**B and C**).

2 Tewin to Codicote

At the green continue forward (signposted Burnham Green) for ½ mile and then turn right just before the Plume of Feathers PH (Tewin Hill) to Queen Hoo Hall (**D**). The lane bears sharp left by the Hall, then take the right fork to a T-junction, turning left (**E**) to BULLS

GREEN and on to DATCHWORTH GREEN. At the crossroads turn left (**F**) and continue forward to WOOLMER GREEN. Turn right on the B197 and soon turn left into Bridge Road. At the top of the hill turn left to cross the motorway and after ½ mile turn right to RABLEY HEATH and CODICOTE (**G**).

3   Codicote to near Ayot Green
In Codicote turn right on the B656 and immediately left along Cowards Lane and again left into St Albans Road. Descend the hill to cross the River Mimram and at a crossroads continue forward for 2½ miles towards Wheathampstead. Approaching this village, after the second lane to Ayot St Lawrence (**H**), look for a bridleway on the left by some large green gates. Take the bridleway, stony but rideable, and descend for ½ mile to a point (just before an underpass), where a former railway crossed (**I**). Turn left through a gate and follow the bridleway (**J**) for 2½ miles.

4   Ayot Green to Stanborough
At the end descend to the road and turn right (signposted Little Green). Soon at a T-junction (unsigned) turn right via a narrow, twisting lane to eventually descend to the ford at WATEREND. Beyond the bridged ford turn right on the B653 and immediately left to COLEMAN GREEN (**K**). Just beyond this hamlet turn left into Tower Hill Lane and at the end left again into Hammonds Lane to follow the edge of Symondshyde Great Wood (**L**). At a T-junction (signposted Welwyn Garden City, Hatfield) turn left and soon left again and continue forward to STANBOROUGH.

Shaw's Corner, Ayot St Lawrence

5 Stanborough to Welwyn Garden City

At a roundabout near the motorway continue forward with care to enter WELWYN GARDEN CITY via Stanborough Road (M). At the first roundabout bear left into Parkway for ½ mile, when the station is signposted to the right via Howardsgate.

Short Cut

To omit 7 miles – from Ayot Green to Welwyn Garden City
In Section 3, nearly a mile after the crossroads below Codicote, turn left to Ayot St Peter and Little Green. At a T-junction (where the main ride continues to the right) continue straight on to AYOT GREEN. Cross a motorway bridge to the B197 and turn right. (*Take care – there is much fast-moving traffic on this road*). After 1 mile, at the foot of the hill, turn left into Valley Road to enter WELWYN GARDEN CITY. Near the top, turn right into Russellcroft Road, cross Parkway using the footpath near the fountain, and continue ahead to the station.

Alternative start and finish – Hatfield

Start
From HATFIELD Station car park use the footbridge to cross the railway, and then turn right into Beaconsfield Road. At a roundabout continue forward into Ground Lane to the next roundabout, at which take the first exit – Birchwood Avenue. At the very end use the underpass at half left to cross the road and the motorway. Beyond the underpass use the footpath to the right to Manor Road where turn left and immediately right by some shops in Green Lanes. Continue forward for a mile to a small roundabout where take the third exit towards Stanborough, to join the main ride at the end of Section 4.

Finish
In Section 4, after Symondshyde Great Wood and the left turn towards Welwyn Garden City soon turn right into Manor Road. Just before a large roundabout use the underpass at half-right to cross the motorway and the road. At the far end turn left and right into Birchwood Avenue. At the second roundabout take the third exit (Homestead Road which becomes Ground Lane). At a roundabout continue forward into Beaconsfield Road. After ¼ mile, near some factories on the left is a footpath leading to the station.

Points of Interest

A   Welwyn Garden City   Started some 20 years later than Letchworth (the First Garden City) and subsequently developed as a New Town (not the same thing). Tourist Information Centre at the

Library on Campus West – a short distance from the Cherry Tree PH on Bridge Road

B   *Tewin*   St Peter's churchyard, just before entering village, grave of Lady Ann Grimston, died 1717. She is said to have claimed that if there were a God, seven trees would spring from her grave – which they did

C   *Tewin – Nature trail*   3½ miles, starts and finishes at Rose and Crown Inn, Lower Green. Guide available from Tewin Post Office

D   *Queen Hoo Hall*   Magnificent Jacobean building, no longer open to the public, but visible from the road

E   *Clibbons post*   Soon after the left turn towards Datchworth. On the left of the road is a post, placed there in 1927 by the East Herts. Archaeological Society. It marks the spot where local men dealt with a highwayman, Walter Clibbon, in 1782. He was done to death and buried with a stake through his heart to prevent him causing any further trouble.

F   *Datchworth Green*   To the left is a whipping post – no longer used, we understand!

G   *Codicote*   A village is known to have existed here before the Norman Conquest. The village contains many old houses in addition to the more obvious recent developments

H   *Ayot St Lawrence – Shaw's Corner*   Home of playwright George Bernard Shaw from 1906 to 1950. Downstairs rooms kept as used by G.B.S.

I   *Wheathampstead – Devil's Dyke*   A little way ahead, beyond the underpass is a ford, from which can be seen ½ mile ahead, an enormous Belgic (pre-Roman) fortress. Free access at all times. The track ahead is rideable and leads to a public road which goes up to Devil's Dyke

J   *The Ayot Greenway*   A former rail track, now a footpath and bridleway. It should be rideable in spite of one or two muddy spots after rain. If riders have any doubts, then they should approach WATEREND by taking the first left turn (signposted Ayot St Peter) beyond the crossroads mentioned at Section 3. After 2 miles this reaches the signpost 'Little Green' referred to at Section 4

K   *Coleman Green*   The John Bunyan Inn reminds us that the non-conformist preacher was active here

L   *Symondshyde Great Wood*   Ancient wood with picnic area

M   *Stanborough Lakes*   Sailing lakes and swimming pool. Nature conservation area

RIDE No 16

A Circuit of St Albans

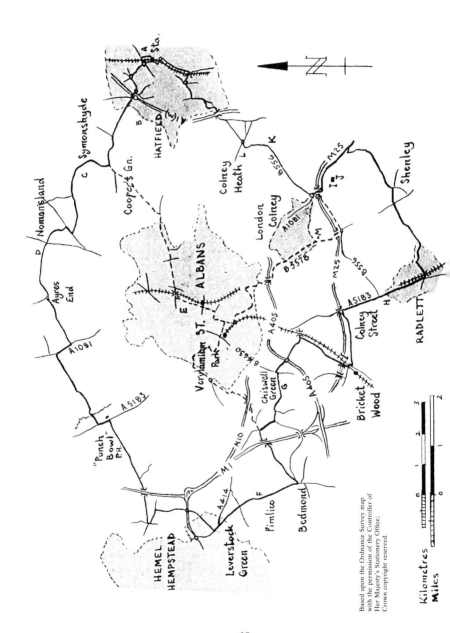

Kilometres
Miles

This ride comprises a circuit of St Albans, one of the country's most historic cities. It includes much easy riding in lanes which run through some of the delightful countryside which remains between the four large towns of Hatfield, St Albans, Hemel Hempstead and Watford. A route through the city is mentioned which avoids much of the busy city centre, but obviously such an ancient city is busy with motor traffic at most times. There is far too much in St Albans to see in one day, but we mention some of the more important places.

Amongst the interesting places outside St Albans is a museum where the development took place during World War 2 of a revolutionary aircraft, the de Havilland Mosquito. On a more peaceful note, the ride passes the Gardens of the Rose, where 1700 varieties, the nations favourite flowers, are on display. We also encounter a number of Coal Posts – reminders of the Great Fire of London in 1666

Map: Sheet 166 in the O.S. Landranger series

Based on Hatfield – 32 miles (alternatively 25 or 16 miles)
Alternatively from Welwyn Garden City – add 2 miles; from St Albans – 34, 30, 22 or 16 miles; Hemel Hempstead or Watford – 40, 36 or 25 miles; Radlett – 32, 26 or 20 miles

1   Hatfield to Symondshyde turn
Leave HATFIELD Station (**A**), to cross the car park on the right. Use the footbridge to cross the railway, and then turn right into Beaconsfield Road. At a roundabout continue forward into Ground Lane to the next roundabout at which turn left into Birchwood Avenue. At the very end use the underpass at half-left to cross the road and the motorway. Beyond the underpass use the footpath to the right to Manor Road (**B**), where turn left to the end. At Coopers Green Lane turn left and continue forward for ½ mile to a lane to the right – Hammond Lane (signposted Symonshyde).

2   Symondshyde to Harpenden
Turn right into Hammond Lane, past Symondshyde Great Wood (**C**) on the left and continue forward past Hammonds Farm to descend to a T-junction. Here turn right (signposted Coleman Green) and soon left (signposted Wheathamstead) to a crossroads with the B651. Continue straight on to cross NOMANSLAND COMMON (**D**) to AYRES END. At a triangle turn left and continue forward to a T-junction with the A1081. Turn right towards Harpenden for a short way to a left turn (Beesonend Lane).

3   Harpenden to Bedmond
Turn left and soon left again (Beesonend Lane) to avoid the housing estate, and then continue forward past Redbournbury and two bridged fords across the River Ver, to a T-junction with the A5183. Turn left towards St Albans for ½ mile to the Punch Bowl PH. Here

69

turn right into Punch Bowl Lane and continue forward for 2 miles to a T-junction with Cherrytrees Lane. Turn left into Cherrytrees Lane and soon left again, past the oil depot. Follow the lane to the right at a corner (Green Lane, not signed) and continue forward to a roundabout on the A414 opposite the BP offices. Take the second exit and continue forward on the narrow Green Lane to a T-junction with Leverstock Green Road. Turn left and soon right into Bedmond Road for 2 miles through PIMLICO (**F**) to BEDMOND.

4 Bedmond to Radlett
At the top of Church Hill turn sharp left next to a small church into Serge Hill Lane. Soon continue forward in St Albans Lane which becomes Bedmond Lane, to POTTERS CROUCH. At a crossroads turn right into Blunts Lane and soon, at a T-junction turn left. Soon again at a crossroads continue forward along Chiswell Green Lane to BONE HILL (**G**) and CHISWELL GREEN to the junction with the B4630. Turn left with care and immediately right into Tippendell Lane and forward to a roundabout on the A405. Continue forward with great care (*much fast traffic*) into Tippendell Lane and forward for ½ mile to PARK STREET. Turn right BEFORE the rail bridge into Park Street Lane and continue forward for 1½ miles to SMUG OAK where turn sharp left by The Gate PH (Smug Oak Lane). Continue forward for 1 mile to COLNEY STREET, and the junction with the A5183. Turn right onto the A5183 and continue forward for 2 miles to RADLETT (**H**). The A5183 can be avoided by using about 1 mile of bridleways, only a small section of which is rough. At the Gate, keep forward in Station Road for ½ mile. Left into School Lane for ¾ mile. At a bridleway sign turn left for ¼ mile. At another bridleway sign fork left, soon to pass through a gate. Forward to cross a river footbridge and forward to go through another gate. Turn right and soon left to climb a hill. At the top turn right to Blackbirds Farm. Bear left on a metalled road to the end. Turn right into Kemprow to High Cross. Left and soon left again on B462 to Radlett. At A5183 turn right to rail station.

5 Radlett to the Bell Inn roundabout
Turn left next to the rail station and climb Shenley Hill to SHENLEY crossroads. Continue forward into Rectory Lane and soon turn left to RIDGE HILL, to a junction with the A1081. Turn left (**I and J**) and descend to a roundabout near the M25. Take the second exit to the BELL INN roundabout.

6 The Bell Inn roundabout to Hatfield

Take the fourth exit the B556, Coursers Road. (*You may prefer to walk direct to this exit.*) Follow this road (**K**) to COLNEY HEATH (**L**). At a small roundabout continue forward into Roestock Lane (signed 'No through road') and at the end use the cycle-track underpass to cross the A1(M). At the end of the cycle-track turn sharp right to take a footpath (Lane End) to Hazel Grove, where turn left to the end. Turn left into Bishops Rise and at the first roundabout take the third exit (Woods Avenue). At the next roundabout take the second exit (Oxlease Drive) to the end. Turn left on the A1000 for ½ mile to a roundabout, where take the second exit to Hatfield Station.

Short Cuts

1 From Symondshyde to St Albans City Centre and return to Hatfield in 16 miles

1.1 At the end of Section 1 of the main ride continue forward to the end of Coopers Green Lane, where turn right into Sandpit Lane for 1½ miles until just beyond the rail bridge. Turn left into Lemsford Road and continue forward into Beaconsfield Road (**E**).

1.2 At the end, ST ALBANS City Station is to the left (Victoria Street). If this is not your destination, cross Victoria Street, continue forward into Alma Road, and cross London Road. Continue forward into Black Cut to reach Old London Road, where turn right.

1.3 Soon a choice exists. At a crossroads, either continue forward into Albert Street, to reach Holywell Hill. Sumpter Yard on the far side leads to the Cathedral, Verulamium and beyond to Kingsbury Water Mill museum, about 1 mile away. Alternatively, at the crossroads, turn left into Cottonmill Lane and continue forward for 1 mile, past Sopwell House, to a roundabout. Take the second exit (Napsbury Lane) and forward to cross the North Orbital Road by a bridge to join the B5378.

1.4 Continue forward for 2 miles, past London Colney (**M**) and over the M25 to a roundabout. Take the first exit and soon, at another roundabout follow the signs to COLNEY HEATH, to rejoin the main ride at Section 6.

2 From Potters Crouch to return to Hatfield via St Albans City Centre – 25 miles

2.1 At POTTERS CROUCH crossroads in Section 4, continue forward for 100 yards to fork left by the Holly Bush PH for 1½ miles to join the A4147. Turn right to a roundabout and continue forward on the A4147.

2.2 Descend and soon turn right into St Michaels Street. After 200 yards turn right into Verulam Park at the museum.

2.3 Cross the park (walking) to emerge at the foot of Holywell Hill near the Abbey Station.

2.4 Cross to Prospect Road and continue forward. At the end turn left into Cottonmill Lane for ¼ mile and then turn right into Old London Road. Soon turn left into Black Cut and continue forward into Alma Road to Victoria Street near the City Station.

2.5 Continue forward into Beaconsfield Road and Lemsford Road to Sandpit Lane. Here turn right for 1½ miles to a roundabout. Take the first exit (Coopers Green Lane) and continue forward for 2 miles. At Manor Road turn right and continue to the end.

2.6 Cross the motorway using the subway to the right. At the far end turn left and right into Birchwood Avenue. At the second roundabout take the third exit (Homestead Road which becomes Ground Lane). At a roundabout continue forward into Beaconsfield Road. Near some factories on the left take the footpath over the railway to HATFIELD Station.

Alternative starts and finishes

1 St Albans
1.1 St Albans/Hatfield – 16, 30 or 41 miles
From ST ALBANS City Station follow Short Cut 1 (above) from Section 1.2 through Sections 1.3 and 1.4 as far as the BELL INN roundabout. Then follow the main ride Sections 5, 6 and 1, returning to St Albans via Sandpit Lane as per Short Cut 1. This gives a circuit of 16 miles.

By continuing the main ride from Symondshyde to Hemel Hempstead and returning to St Albans from Potters Crouch via Short Cut 2 gives a circuit of 30 miles.

As an alternative to returning from POTTERS CROUCH, the main ride can be followed to near the end of Section 5, to the roundabout close to the M25, just beyond Salisbury Hall. Turn left on the B556 to the next roundabout, take the third exit (B5378). Continue past LONDON COLNEY (**M**) for 2 miles to cross the

St Albans - The Fighting Cocks

North Orbital Road by a bridge, and then continue forward in Napsbury Lane. At a roundabout take the first exit, Cottonmill Lane. Soon after crossing the River Ver at 1 mile, turn right into Old London Road and then left into Black Cut. Cross London Road and continue forward in Alma Road. The City Station is to the right in Victoria Street giving a total ride of 41 miles.

1.2   St Albans/Hemel Hempstead – 34 or 22 miles

From ST ALBANS City Station take Beaconsfield Road, which becomes Lemsford Road to the end. Turn right into Sandpit Lane for 1½ miles to a small roundabout. Take the first exit (Coopers Green Lane). Continue forward for 2 miles, and then turn left into Hammonds Lane to join the main ride at Section 2. Return to St Albans may be either from Potters Crouch (see Short Cut 2) or from London Colney (see 1.1 St Albans/Hatfield above).

2.   Hemel Hempstead

Since this ride passes through Leverstock Green there are a number of possibilities for joining and leaving it in Hemel Hempstead. The A414 is a road to be avoided, and the roundabout near the Town Centre would not be our choice for riding or walking or even driving. The quietest link from the station is undoubtedly the canal towpath, as described, but, even with a licence, cycling is not permitted between bridges 148 and 152 (Old Fishery Lane and Durrants Hill Road by the Albion PH).

Three possible uses of this circuit (with distances from the station) are as follows.

1 Follow the complete circuit via Hatfield (40 miles).
2 Ride the southern part through Hatfield as far as Coopers
   Green Lane and then return through St Albans and Potters
   Crouch (Short Cut 2 in reverse) making 36 miles.
3 Use Short Cut 2 (above) from Potters Crouch to St Albans
   and then ride the '1.2 St Albans/Hemel Hempstead' route
   above (25 miles).

Start
Leave HEMEL HEMPSTEAD Station yard and go forward in Fishery Road to the canal at the Fishery Inn. Join the towpath on the
left, pass under the bridge and continue for 2 miles to Red Lion
Lane at Nash Mills. Turn left into Red Lion Lane to the end and
then left again into Lower Road and soon turn right into Bunkers
Lane for 1½ miles to its end. Turn right to PIMLICO to join main
ride in Section 3.

*A rideable alternative, but which can often be busier with traffic than
we would find comfortable, is as follows.*
From Fishery Road, just beyond the canal, turn right into Kingsland
Road to its end. Turn left and right into St Johns Road. At the end
cross Station Road, continue forward on an unsigned road to cross
Two Waters Road and again forward in Corner Hall to Lawn Lane.
Turn right and follow Lawn Lane and Belswains Lane for 1½ miles
until a left turn named Bunkers Road. Here turn left for 1½ miles
to the end and then right to join the main ride in Section 3. At Two
Waters Road or Durrants Hill Road there are opportunities to join
the canal towpath to the right.

Finish
Beyond Leverstock Green in Section 3, turn right into Bunkers
Lane. At the bottom turn left and soon right into Red Lion Lane.
At the canal take the towpath to the right for 2 miles to the Fishery
Inn. Leave the towpath to take Fishery Road to the station.
Alternatively, at the bottom of Bunkers Lane turn right into
Belswains Lane which becomes Lawn Lane, for 1½ miles. Soon
after a descending right bend, turn left into Corner Hall. Go forward
to cross Two Water Road and to Station Road. Turn left and immediately right into St Johns Road. At the end of the green on the left,
turn left into Wharf Road and right into Kingsland Road. At the
end turn left into Fishery Road to the station.

3 From Welwyn Garden City – add 2 miles to Hatfield distances
Start
From the front of WELWYN GARDEN CITY Station turn right
into Stonehills to a roundabout. Take the second exit (Bridge Road
– B195) for ½ mile. Turn left into Valley Road (B195) and continue

74

forward to the bottom. At a roundabout take the second exit to pass under the motorway. At a second roundabout take the third exit to LEMSFORD. Beyond the village, at the B653, turn right and immediately left into Green Lanes and continue to a roundabout. Here take the third exit (Coopers Green Lane) to join the main ride near the end of Section 1.

Finish
At Manor Road in Section 1, turn right into Green Lanes to a roundabout. Take the third exit to enter Welwyn Garden City by STANBOROUGH. At a roundabout beyond the motorway take the first exit (Stanborough Road). At the next roundabout bear left into Parkway for ½ mile. The station is signposted to the right via Howardsgate.

4 Watford – distances are the same as for Hemel Hempstead
Start and finish
Leave WATFORD Junction Station and ride to and from BEDMOND, Church Hill, as described in ride No 20. Join this ride at Section 4.

Three possible rides are as described above under Hemel Hempstead.

5 Radlett
There are three possible uses of this circuit starting at RADLETT Station in Section 5.
 i) The full circuit as described (32 miles).
 ii) Via Hatfield to Symondshyde and then to St Albans using Short Cut No 1; from St Albans to Potters Crouch using Short Cut No 2 (Sections 2.1 to 2.4 in reverse) and then rejoin the main ride in Section 4 (26 miles).
 iii) To the Bell Inn (Section 5) and then to St Albans as described under 'St Albans/Hatfield (1.1)' above; then to Potters Crouch and rejoin the main ride in Section 4 (20 miles).

Points of Interest

A Hatfield House Home of the Marquess of Salisbury. A Jacobean House and Tudor palace; the childhood home of Queen Elizabeth I. Open to the public in the summer

B Hatfield Aerodrome Owned by British Aerospace. Not open to the public, but it is possible to see new and interesting aircraft being tested overhead

C Symondshyde Great Wood Picnic area

D Nomansland Common Heathland with nature trail starting

75

near the cricket pavilion opposite The Wicked Lady PH. The name of the area derives from its position as dividing land between the domains of the Abbots of St Albans and Westminster

E *St Albans City* Many places of interest. Cathedral and abbey church of St Alban: first martyr of England, which includes Saxon and Norman work. Verulamium: Roman town with theatre, hypocaust, and parts of city walls from 200 AD Museum. City museum, Hatfield Road. Clock Tower, erected 1402–11. Kingsbury Water Mill museum. Old Fighting Cocks Inn, shaped like a cockpit

F *Pimlico – The Swan* A public house with warplanes and an anti-aircraft gun in the gardens. Also sells beer worth drinking

G *Chiswell Green – The Gardens of the Rose* Headquarters of the Royal National Rose Society. The gardens contain nearly 1700 different varieties of rose and are open to the public in the summer

H *Radlett – outside the Radlett Hall* On the right side of the road, soon after entering Radlett is a London Coal Duty Boundary marker post. This white post with the crest of the Corporation of the City of London is one of a series across the south of the county. They indicate the area within which the Corporation could levy a duty on coal and wine brought in. The duty was originally imposed in 1667 to help rebuild the City after the Great Fire and was levied at 20 miles from the City. In 1861 the boundary was changed to where the existing posts are situated. The duty was abolished in 1889

I *Salisbury Hall* Moated manor house rebuilt in Tudor times on the site of a much older house. Not now open to the public. At one time it numbered Charles II and Nell Gwynne amongst its visitors. More recently (1905 to 1910) it was owned by the mother of Sir Winston Churchill. In the 1930s it was the home of Sir Nigel Gresley, designer of many steam locomotives and in particular 'Mallard' which set the world speed record in 1938

J *Mosquito museum* Adjacent to Salisbury Hall. The design and initial development took place here in World War 2 of the de Havilland Mosquito aircraft. A museum devoted to this and also to aircraft engines is in the hangar

K *Coursers Lane – near Coursers Farm* On the right side of the road, on a bend is a Coal Post

L *Colney Heath* On the left, behind The Queens Head PH is a Coal Post. Not far away, in the High Street and opposite the Cock PH is another

M *London Colney* South side of Broad Colney bridge (at the south end of the village). Another Coal Post

RIDE No 17

West Herts Between the Gade and the Upper Lea

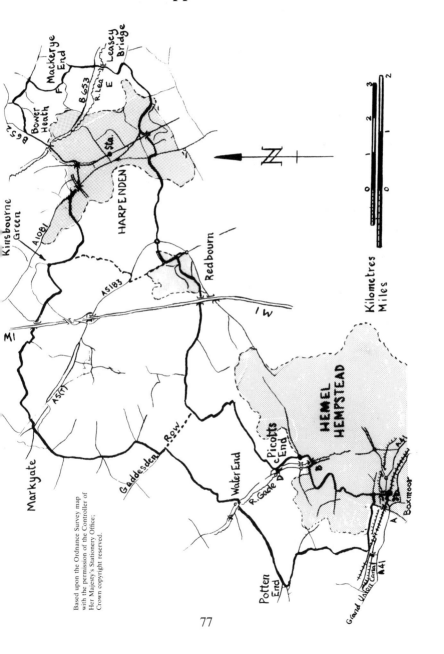

This circuit explores some of the mixed countryside tucked away between Hemel Hempstead and Luton. It also fringes the pleasant town of Harpenden. The ride starts by the River Bulbourne and the Grand Union Canal. It then crosses some high ground to descend to the infant River Ver, from which the Roman Verulamium took its name, and then visits the upper valley of the River Lea. The return is via Gaddesden Row, which has a remoteness about it, although it is so close to two major towns

Map: Sheet 166 in the O.S. Landranger series

Based on Hemel Hempstead – 31 miles (alternatively – 23 or 13 miles)

Alternatively from Harpenden – 32, 26, 22 or 16 miles

1   Hemel Hempstead to Gaddesden Row (Corner Farm)

From HEMEL HEMPSTEAD Station cross the A41 with care and continue forward in Fishery Road (**A**). At a roundabout take the second exit (Green End Road). At the top continue ahead on a footpath to Gravel Lane. Turn right and then continue to the top. Near a Scout HQ continue forward on a footpath (parallel to the busy Warners End Road) to Melsted Road. Continue to the end of Melsted Road and then turn left to cross Warners End Road to Gadebridge Road. Continue forward for ¼ mile, then turn right into Gadebridge Lane. At Leighton Buzzard Road turn right and soon left to continue in Gadebridge Lane (**B**). At the end turn left into Piccotts End Road to PICCOTTS END village (**C and D**). Beyond the village and shortly before the A4146, turn right into Dodds Lane for nearly 2 miles to a T-junction. Turn left (signposted Jockey End) to a junction by Corner Farm.

2   Gaddesden Row to South Harpenden

At Corner Farm turn right and continue forward to descend gently by a twisting lane to REDBOURN. Just after passing under the M1, at a T-junction turn left to cross the Common and to reach the High Street. Turn left along the High Street and at a roundabout take the third exit (Harpenden Lane). Continue forward to cross the infant River Ver, and at a roundabout take the second exit (B487) to HARPENDEN.

3   South Harpenden to Mackerye End

At the A1081 turn right towards St Albans and soon turn left in Cravells Road. At the bottom, at a roundabout take the third exit, Grove Road. At the next roundabout continue forward and soon turn left into Pipers Lane (signposted Wheathampstead) to a T-junction with a fine view over the Upper Lea valley. Turn left and soon right into Leasey Bridge Lane to descend and to cross an old rail track and the River Lea (**E**) to reach the B653. Cross this road

Mackerye House

and continue forward for ½ mile to MARSHALLS HEATH. At the top of a hill turn left to MACKERYE END (**F**).

4 Mackerye End to Kinsbourne Green

Continue forward to a crossroads. Turn left into Sauncy Wood Lane and soon right into Holly Lane. At the bottom (*take care on the descent*), turn left and soon right to emerge on the B652 at BOWER HEATH. Turn left and descend to a crossroads with the B653. Continue forward into Westfield Road for ½ mile, and then turn right over the railway into Hollybush Lane to descend to the A1081, Luton Road. Turn right for ¼ mile to The Old Bell PH and then turn left into Roundwood Lane. After 1 mile turn right to KINSBOURNE GREEN crossroads.

5 Kinsbourne Green to Water End

Turn left into Annables Lane (signposted Flamstead) and after 1 mile turn right (signposted Pepperstock). Then continue forward in Gibraltar Lane, under the M1 to a T-junction where turn right (signposted Pepperstock) and soon turn left to MARKYATE. (*Care on a twisting descent followed by a climb, and on the final descent to the bypass.*) Cross the A5 and the High Street and keep forward in Pickford Road to climb to CHEVERELLS GREEN. Continue forward for 2 miles to a T-junction where turn left (Gaddesden Row) and immediately right for nearly 2 miles to WATER END.

6 Water End to Hemel Hempstead

Turn right on the A4146 and immediately left to POTTEN END. Turn left opposite the church (The Green) and left again in Hempstead Lane. After ¾ mile turn right into Pouchen End Lane, and then keep forward for 1½ miles. At the foot of a hill, just before a railway bridge, turn left into Chaulden Lane. At the end turn right into Old Fishery Lane (signposted 'No Through Road'). Cross the canal and pass through some gates to the A41. Turn left for 300 yards to the station. If the A41 traffic is heavy, as is usual, there is a good footpath.

Short Cuts

1 To omit 18 miles – From Corner Farm, to return to Hemel Hempstead via Water End
At Corner Farm at the end of Section 1, turn left for 1 mile, and then left again (signposted Water End) to rejoin the main ride at Section 6.

2 To omit 8 miles – From Redbourn to Kinsbourne Green
At Redbourn High Street in Section 2, continue forward to join the A5183. Turn right and soon left to Kinsbourne Green. Rejoin the main ride at the end of Section 4.

Alternative start and finish from Harpenden

The full circuit is 32 miles, but omitting Hemel Hempstead makes 22 miles. Omitting the detour via Mackerye End is 6 miles less.

Grand Union Canal, Hemel H...

Start

From HARPENDEN Station car park, cross Station Road and go forward in Carlton Road to the end, and then turn right into Sun Lane. Soon turn left into Hollybush Lane to join the main ride in Section 4.

Finish

In Section 4 (Westfield Road), instead of turning right into Hollybush Lane, continue forward and then turn left into Carlton Road to the station.

Alternatively, at the end of Section 2, just before the A1081, turn left via a drive and footpath parallel to the A1081 to Leyton Road. Pass Rothamsted Experimental Station and continue forward to emerge on the busy High Street opposite the Harpenden Inn. The station is a short way along Station Road.

To omit Hemel Hempstead

At GADDESDEN ROW (near the end of Section 5), turn left and continue forward to Corner Farm. Turn left to join the main ride at Section 2.

Points of Interest

A Boxmoor – The Fishery Inn   A canal-side inn which is proud of its age, and which displays canal mileages. It once had stabling for 40 horses, when the canal was an important means of transport

B Gadebridge Park   Gade Valley nature trail is open all year. Note the attractively styled iron bridge to the right, built in 1840

C Piccott's End – No 136   15th century wall paintings and museum in a building believed to have been a pilgrims' hospice. It also contains a priest's hiding hole, a medieval well and a collection of historical medical equipment. In more recent times it became the first cottage hospital in England
NOTE. Although this building may reopen to the public in 1989, at the time of writing it is an antiques business and is NOT open for public viewing

D Piccotts End   Weatherboarded mill on 18th century brick, with 18th century mill house adjacent

E Harpenden – Upper Lea Valley Through Walk   Continuous walk between Leasey Bridge and Westfield Road. Constructed by Upper Lea Valley Group

F Mackerye End   Written about by Charles Lamb, whose great-aunt lived here

RIDE No 18

Canal Views, Commons and Chiltern Beeches

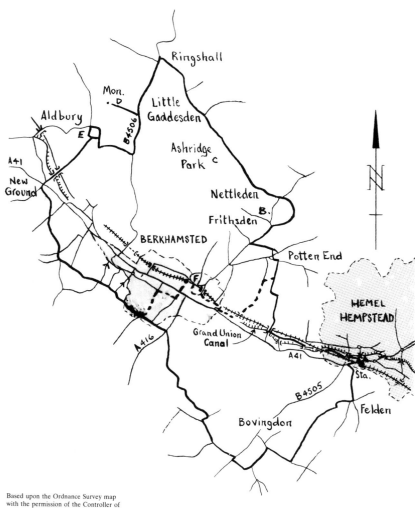

Based upon the Ordnance Survey map
with the permission of the Controller of
Her Majesty's Stationery Office;
Crown copyright reserved.

A mixture of canal views, open commons, woodlands and Chiltern beeches. This ride includes some of the highest ground in the county without being excessively hilly. We encounter a 16th century canal-side inn, a vineyard, and a monument to a canal builder. It does include one steep hill on the return journey, which takes us briefly out of the county into Buckinghamshire.

The A41 road is not recommended as a short cut on the return journey. Please see the note at the front of this book regarding cycling on canal towpaths

Map: Sheets 165 and 166 in the O.S. Landranger series

Based on Hemel Hempstead – 25 miles (alternatively – 14 miles)
Alternatively from Berkhamsted – 27 or 13 miles; or Tring – 25 miles

1 Hemel Hempstead to Potten End

Leave HEMEL HEMPSTEAD Station and cross the A41 to Fishery Road. Continue forward to the canal bridge (**A**), and turn left along the towpath for 1 mile to the 16th-century Three Horseshoes Inn. Cross the swing bridge and soon turn left into Pix Farm Lane. At the end turn right into Little Heath Lane to POTTEN END. At a T-junction turn left to the Common.

Those who do not care for towpath riding can follow Fishery Road to a roundabout and then turn left into Northridge Way. Soon turn left into Chaulden Lane and at the end turn left and right to join Pix Farm Lane. Continue forward to POTTEN END as described above.

2 Potten End to Aldbury

At the Common, just before the Red Lion PH, turn right (signposted Water End, Great Gaddesden) and soon at a crossroads continue forward to the end. Turn left into Vicarage Road to the end and then turn right to descend gently (**B**) to NETTLEDEN. Continue forward for 3½ miles through LITTLE GADDESDEN and to RINGSHALL. Turn left on the B4506 (signposted Berkhamsted), through the Ashridge Estate (**C**).

After 1 mile, detour right to the Bridgewater Monument (**D**) and rejoin the B4506. After a further ¾ mile turn right to descend steeply to ALDBURY (**E**).

3 Aldbury to Bovingdon

Leave the village by Trooper Road to NEW GROUND. Cross the A41 with care and continue forward in Hemp Lane towards Wigginton. Almost immediately, turn left in an unsigned lane and after a climb, turn left near the rear entrance to Champneys, and then continue forward to enter BERKHAMSTED via Shootersway.

Ashbury

When this road joins the A416, continue forward for ¼ mile. Just after a roundabout, turn left (signposted Haresfoot Farm). Continue forward for 3 miles, climbing White Hill on the way, to join the B4505. At the B4505 turn left towards Bovingdon, and then soon turn right and left (signposted Bovingdon Green) to enter BOVINGDON.

4 Bovingdon to Hemel Hempstead
In the village turn right towards Chipperfield and at the speed dere-striction sign turn left into an unsigned lane to FELDEN. In Felden turn left and soon left again to descend Felden Lane to the A41. The station is 200 yards to the right.

Short Cut

To omit 11 miles – from Potten End to Berkhamsted
In Section 1, just before POTTEN END, turn left (signposted Berk-hamsted) and soon, at a crossroads, continue forward to descend to BERKHAMSTED. Just after crossing the canal turn right into Bank Mill Lane as far as the speed limit signs. Turn right to re-cross the canal and forward to a T-junction with Ivy House Lane. Turn left and then right to Station Road (**F**). Continue forward into Lower Kings Road to the traffic lights on the A41. Continue forward into Kings Road and soon turn right into Charles Street. After ½ mile turn left into Cross Oak Road to the top. Here turn left into Shoot-ersway for ½ mile to join the A416. Rejoin the main ride in Section 3.

Alternative starts and finish points

1 Berkhamsted
From BERKHAMSTED Station turn right into Lower Kings Road and follow the notes under 'short cut' above, returning either from Potten End as described under 'short cut', or making the complete circuit and returning to Berkhamsted from Shootersway via the A416 (Kings Road) to the High Street and Lower Kings Road.

2 Tring
Start
Leave TRING Station and turn left. Soon, after crossing the canal in a deep cutting, turn left (signposted Berkhamsted) to NEW GROUND, to join the main ride in Section 3.

Finish
At Section 3, (in Aldbury) continue forward on Station Road for 1 mile to TRING Station.

Points of Interest

A Boxmoor – The Fishery Inn   A fine canal-side inn which proudly declares its age and shows canal mileages on its front. In the great days of canals it had stabling for 40 horses

B Frithsden – Roman Road   Vineyard established in 1972. Open to the public in the summer and autumn

C Ashridge House   The present building was constructed in 1808 as a romantic 'Gothic' mansion by James Wyatt for the 3rd Earl of Bridgewater. It now houses Ashridge Management College. An earlier house was visited by Henry VIII and Elizabeth I. The gardens which were originally laid out by Capability Brown (though later altered) are open to the public in the summer

D Bridgewater Monument   Off the road to the right. Erected in 1832 to commemorate the canal building feats of the 3rd Duke of Bridgewater. Open to visitors in the summer. Nature trail and information centre

E Aldbury   A picturesque village complete with stocks on the village green, a pond and many old cottages. As we move away from the village, it is worth looking back to see the background of trees against which this fine village is set

F Berkhamsted Castle   Consists of a Norman motte and bailey earthworks with later stone walls. William the Conqueror camped here

RIDE No 19

The Far West

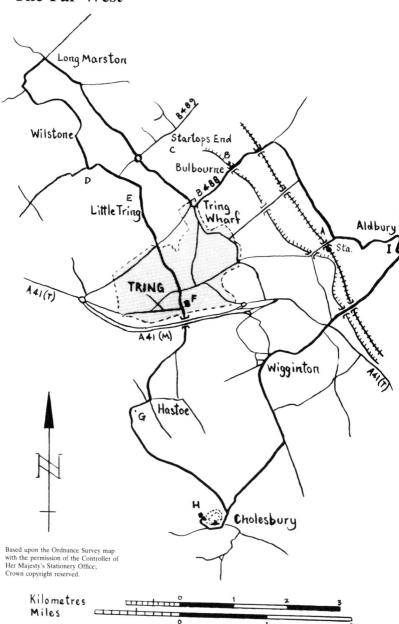

Based upon the Ordnance Survey map
with the permission of the Controller of
Her Majesty's Stationery Office;
Crown copyright reserved.

86

This short ride includes a remarkable contrast in landscapes. It starts with some miles of easy pedalling in flat, open country with views of the Grand Union Canal and its reservoirs, now designated as nature reserves. The only hills are the bridges over the canal. In the second part of the ride we reach the highest point in the county at over 800 feet above sea level, followed by a nice descent through a tree-lined lane which forms the county boundary with Buckinghamshire.

This ride reveals many old cottages tucked away in villages. We see a British Waterways works where lock gates are made, and a dry dock for narrow boats. We detour a short way into Buckinghamshire to see an Iron Age fort of considerable proportions and finally the picture-postcard village of Aldbury, which still has the stocks on the village green

Map: Sheet 165 in the O.S. Landranger series

Based on Tring – 18 miles
Alternatively from Berkhamsted – 29 miles

1 Tring to Long Marston

From TRING Station **(A)** turn right towards Aldbury and soon turn left (signposted Pitstone, Ivinghoe) for 1½ miles. At a T-junction with the B488 turn left for 1½ miles through BULBOURNE **(B)** to

Bulbourne

Tring Reservoir

TRING WHARF. At an unusual road junction turn right and right again (Gamnel Terrace). Then continue forward for 2½ miles (**C**) to LONG MARSTON.

2 Long Marston to Cholesbury

Turn left opposite the Queens Head PH into Astrope Road for ½ mile. Then turn left again into an unsigned lane which bears a notice 'Unsuitable for heavy goods vehicles' to WILSTONE. At Wilstone turn right into Tring Road, and through the village to a T-junction with the B489, which has a reservoir behind an embankment opposite (**D**). Turn left for ½ mile, and where the road bears left, near the cemetery, continue forward on an unsigned lane and on through LITTLE TRING (**E**) to the B488. Continue straight on into Dundale Road which becomes Frogmore Street. At the end cross the High Street and forward into Akeman Street. At the end (**F**) turn right and immediately left under the bypass and soon turn right to HASTOE. Here bear right, to keep on the tarmac road (**G**). Follow Shire Lane, which here forms the county boundary, to its end. Turn right for ¼ mile to CHOLESBURY (Bucks) (**H**).

3 Cholesbury to Tring Station

Retrace out of the village, past the bottom of Shire Lane and continue forward for 1½ miles to a T-junction and turn left to WIGGIN-TON. Turn right by the War Memorial (Hemp Lane, signposted Aldbury) to descend to NEW GROUND. At the foot of the descent cross the A41 and continue forward to ALDBURY (**I**). In the village turn left towards Tring to reach the station.

Alternative start and finish – Berkhamsted
Start
From BERKHAMSTED Station turn right into Lower Kings Road and on to the High Street (A41). Cross at the traffic lights and

forward into Kings Road (A416). Soon turn right into Charles Street for ½ mile and then turn left into Cross Oak Road to its end. Here turn right into Shootersway and continue towards Tring. At the end of a long descent turn right to join the main ride in Section 3 at NEW GROUND.

Finish

In Section 3, near the foot of the descent from WIGGINTON and just before reaching the A41, turn right into an unsigned lane (easily missed) and continue forward to enter BERKHAMSTED by Shootersway. After joining the A416, turn left to descend Kings Road to the High Street (A41). Cross to Lower Kings Road and to the station.

Points of Interest

A   Tring Station   The railway cutting was constructed in 1836/1837 by navvies and horses. It is 2¼ miles long and nearly 60 feet deep. It follows the line of the earlier canal as the flattest path through the Chilterns

B   Bulbourne   Canal and British Waterways workshops. Stylish Victorian buildings where you can look inside and see lock gates being made. Half a mile along the tarmac towpath is a dry dock for narrow boats

C   Startops End   On both sides of the road are reservoirs now designated as nature reserves. They were constructed to supply water for the canal which here reaches a high point on its way through the Chiltern Hills

D   Wilstone   Another reservoir designated as a nature reserve

E   Little Tring   As the road rises it crosses a disused length of canal

F   Tring – Zoological museum, Akeman Street   Natural history exhibits. Established by the 2nd Lord Rothschild as a private collection and now part of the British Museum

G   Hastoe   Just near the left bend, at 802 feet above sea level, is the highest point in the county

H   Cholesbury   As we enter the village, to the left is a common, and to the right, over a double junction and soon right again in Parrotts Lane is the church. This building, of 13th century origin, stands within large earthworks of an Iron Age fort. The ditches and embankment can be clearly seen through a gate to the left of the church drive

I   Aldbury   Standing below the well-wooded ridge is this picturesque village which has many old cottages, a pond and stocks on the village green

89

RIDE No 20

South-West Herts

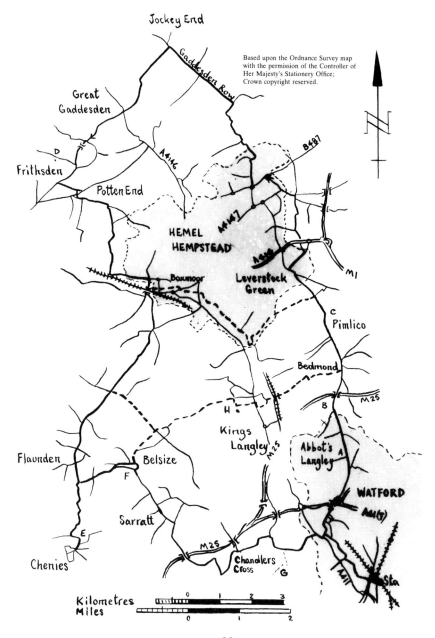

Based upon the Ordnance Survey map with the permission of the Controller of Her Majesty's Stationery Office; Crown copyright reserved.

90

Near to, and easily accessible from the large industrial towns of Wat-
ford and Hemel Hempstead there is some surprising pleasant and
varied countryside. Included are distant views across the Gade and
Bulbourne Valleys, many superb old cottages tucked away in villages;
wooded lanes and open commons, and of course, the Grand Union
Canal.

In the north part of the ride there is even a vineyard at Frithsden.
The western edge of the county is on the fringes of the Chiltern Hills
and on this ride you are invited to cross briefly into Buckinghamshire
to visit the 15th century Chenies Manor, a gem of an English manor
house.

This ride crosses many busy roads such as the A41, A411 and A414
which are not recommended for short cuts

Map: Sheet 166 in the O.S. Landranger series

Based on Watford – 35 miles (alternatively – 32, 25 or 17 miles)
Alternatively from Rickmansworth add 7 miles; or from Chorleywood, add 5 miles
From Hemel Hempstead – 32 miles (alternatively – 23, 22, 18 or 15
miles)

1 Watford to Bedmond
From WATFORD Junction Station turn right into Station Road.
Soon, at some traffic lights, cross St Albans Road (*possibly walking*
this ¼ mile if traffic is heavy). Continue forward into Langley Road,
and after 1 mile turn right by a school into Nascot Wood Road. At
the end continue forward in The Ridgeway and soon turn right into
Courtlands Drive. Continue forward over the A41 by a road bridge
which affords a fine view of Leavesden airfield, to High Road
ABBOTS LANGLEY (**A**). Continue forward via High Road and
then bear left into Hill Farm Avenue, and onward (**B**) to
BEDMOND.

2 Bedmond to Gaddesden Row (Corner Farm)
Continue forward via PIMLICO (**C**) to LEVERSTOCK GREEN.
Turn left onto the A4147 and soon turn right into Green Lane. Soon
after the speed de-restriction sign turn left into Buncefield Lane to
the A414. Cross with care and continue in Buncefield Lane (next to
a petrol filling station) to its end. Turn left into Three Cherry Trees
Lane to a T-junction and here turn right to a roundabout on the
B487. Take the first exit (Redbourn Road) and at the next roundabout take the third exit (St Agnells Lane). Soon, after some schools,

turn right into Cupid Green Lane (signposted Gaddesden Row) and suddenly you are in superb countryside. Bear right at a signpost towards Jockey End, and continue forward past Eastbrook Hay farm to a junction on a road bend at CORNER FARM.

3 Corner Farm to Boxmoor

Turn left and travel along GADDESDEN ROW for nearly 2 miles to near JOCKEY END. Just past Golden Parsonage and a water tower, turn left to GREAT GADDESDEN. Cross the A4146 and the River Gade, go through the village to climb Pipers Hill and then descend to NETTLEDEN. Here turn right and then left (signed 'Unsuitable for motor vehicles'). The lane is rough for a short way, but at the top affords a magnificent view to Ashridge House (right) and Gaddesden Place to the left. Descend to FRITHSDEN (**D**). The village is to the right and worth a detour, but leave to the left, soon to turn right and climb a gentle hill. (*Those who wish to avoid the half mile of rough lane can turn left at Nettleden and soon bear right to rejoin at the exit from Frithsden.*) At the top of the hill turn sharp left to POTTEN END. At a sports ground on the left, turn right into Church Road to cross the Green, and at the end turn left into Hempstead Lane. After ¾ mile turn right into Pouchen End Lane to descend the hill. At the bottom turn left into Chaulden Lane for nearly 1 mile. Near the end turn right into Old Fishery Lane, over the canal and through a rail arch to the A41.

4 Boxmoor to Chipperfield

Turn left on the A41 (*care on this busy road, although there is an ample footpath*) and soon turn right into Felden Lane to FELDEN. Here turn right and then continue forward for 1½ miles to Chipperfield Road. CHIPPERFIELD village, including the common is a worthwhile detour to the left.

5 Chipperfield to Watford

The ride takes us forward over the Chipperfield Road to FLAUNDEN, a small collection of old cottages at a crossroads. Continue forward via a narrow lane to CHENIES (**E**), another worthwhile detour. Retrace up the hill and at the top turn right to BELSIZE (**F**). Continue straight on via Poles Hill to SARRATT where again continue forward to MICKLEFIELD GREEN. Cross the M25 bridge and after 1 mile turn left into Redhall Lane to CHANDLERS CROSS. Continue forward via Fir Tree Hill and after ½ mile turn right into Grove Mill Lane (**G**) to Hempstead Road. Turn right with care and immediately turn left into Courtlands Drive. Soon turn right into The Ridgeway, and continue forward into Nascot Wood Road. At the end turn left into Langley Road. After 1 mile, cross St Albans Road at some traffic lights and continue into Station Road to the station.

Sarratt village green

Short Cuts

1   To omit 3 miles – in Section 5 omit the Chenies detour
At FLAUNDEN, turn left to BELSIZE and continue in Section 5.

2   To omit 10 miles – From Pimlico to Boxmoor
Half a mile beyond PIMLICO, turn left into Bunkers Lane. At the
bottom turn left into Lower Road and soon right into Red Lion
Lane. At the canal, take the towpath to the right and follow this for
2½ miles to a point ¼ mile beyond the Fishery Inn (Bridge 148).
Then take the lane to the left, under the railway arch and through
two gates to the A41. Turn left for a short way and then right into
Felden Lane to rejoin main ride in Section 4. (*Note that a licence is
needed to ride the towpath and that, even so, on 1 mile of the towpath
cycling is not permitted. See also the notes under the alternative finish
to Hemel Hempstead in Ride No 16 – Circuit of St Albans.*)

3   To omit 18 miles – from Bedmond to Belsize
In BEDMOND (the end of Section 1) at the roundabout near the
Bell PH, turn left into Toms Lane to descend to KINGS LANGLEY.
Take care under the railway arch at the bottom, where turn left and
then right into Water Lane. Continue forward to the High Street
(A41) where turn right and soon left into Langley Hill (**H**). At the
end turn left into Chipperfield Road and through CHIPPERFIELD
to BELSIZE. Here turn left to join main ride in Section 5.

Alternative starts and finish points

1   From Hemel Hempstead Station – 32, 23, 22, 18 or 15 miles
A number of circuits are possible. One starting with the north part
of the main circuit (1.1) and three (1.2, 1.3 and 1.4) starting in a
southerly direction.

1.1 Via Piccotts End, Gaddesden Row and Potten End, returning to Boxmoor (15 miles)

Follow Ride No 17 (West Herts), Section 1, to GADDESDEN ROW (Corner Farm) and join this ride at the end of Section 2.

1.2 The full circuit but omitting central Watford (32 or 29 miles)

Leave HEMEL HEMPSTEAD Station and turn left along the A41 (*using the footpath if traffic is heavy*). Soon turn left in Felden Lane to join the main ride at Section 4, leaving it at the same point when finishing. If the Chenies detour is omitted the distance is 3 miles less.

To omit central Watford

At Courtlands Drive in Section 5 continue forward to cross the A41 road bridge and rejoin the main ride in Section 1.

1.3 A short cut from Chipperfield to Bedmond (23 miles)

Start as described in 1.2 above but at Chipperfield Road in Section 4 turn left to CHIPPERFIELD crossroads. Then turn left again via Whippendell Bottom to KINGS LANGLEY. On entering Kings Langley turn right into Langley Hill (**H**) and descend. Turn right on the A41 and soon left into Church Lane, which becomes Water Lane. At the end turn left and then right into Toms Hill to BEDMOND. At Bedmond turn left and follow the main ride from Section 2 or return to BOXMOOR as described in Short Cut 2 above (22 miles).

1.4 From Boxmoor to Pimlico and then the northern part of the ride (22 miles)

Proceed from HEMEL HEMPSTEAD Station to PIMLICO as described in Ride No 16 (Circuit of St Albans) and then join the main ride in Section 2, leaving it at the A41 in Section 4.

2 From Rickmansworth Station, add 7 miles to Watford distances

Start

From RICKMANSWORTH Station forecourt cross the slip road and use the subway to the left to cross the main road. At the end of the subway turn right to Chorleywood Road (A404) – *not recommended for riding – better to walk the footpath*. Soon turn left into Nightingale Road, which becomes The Drive. After ½ mile turn left into Valley Road to its end. Turn right under the M25 and soon right again into Dog Kennel Lane. At the top, cross the A404 and forward for 1½ miles in Solesbridge Lane. At a T-junction turn right to join the main ride in Section 5, near the M25 on the way to CHANDLERS CROSS.

To omit Watford
See note under Hemel Hempstead above.

Finish
Beyond Sarratt, and just after crossing the M25 turn right into Soles-bridge Lane. Continue forward for 1½ miles to the A404 and straight on into Dog Kennel Lane to its end. Turn left and under the M25 and then left into Valley Road to its end. Turn right into The Drive, which becomes Nightingale Road. Continue forward to emerge on the A404, Chorleywood Road. Use the footpath on the right and the subway to reach the station.

3   From Chorleywood Station, add 5 miles to Watford distances
Start
From CHORLEYWOOD Station car park, go forward and at an off-set crossroads turn right and immediately left into Common Gate Road. At the top of the next hill, turn left into Berry Lane and soon left again into Dog Kennel Lane. Read as from the Rickmansworth start (above).

Finish
Read as for finishing to Rickmansworth (above) but at end of Dog Kennel Lane, turn right into Berry Lane. Soon turn right again into Common Gate Road to its end, where turn right and immediately left to the station car park.

Points of Interest

A   Abbot's Langley   Birthplace of Nicholas Breakspear, the only Englishman to become Pope

B   Ovaltine Egg Farm   Just before reaching the M25 bridge

C   Pimlico – The Swan   A public house with warplanes and an anti-aircraft gun in the gardens. Also a childrens playground. The beer is worth drinking too

D   Frithsden – Roman Road, Vineyard   Open to visitors in summer and autumn

E   Chenies   A fine village with a superb manor house open at certain times. The present brick house dates from the 15th century, and is built on a 13th century stone crypt. Home of the Earls of Bedford before they moved to Woburn. Visited by Henry VIII and Elizabeth I. Contains a medieval well and an original Tudor privy

F   Belsize – Olleberrie Lane, Cherry Trees Farm   A working farm open to visitors in summer. Farm museum and tea room

G   Whippendell Wood – Grove Mill Lane   Walks, nature trail and picnic area

H   Kings Langley   Site of a former Royal palace near the top of Langley Hill

The Hertfordshire Wheelers

This book is published as part of the celebrations in 1988 for 60 years of the club's existence. Apart from a few years in World War 2 (when all the members were in HM Forces) it has been active all of that time. Most of the members are between 16 and 30, but some are old enough to have been with the Club 20 years or more. It has a year-round programme of Sunday club runs and social events and members promote and take part in races in the season. If you do think of contacting the club, the Chairman's address is 4, Willowside, London Colney, St Albans, Herts, AL4 1DP, and our clubroom is St Margaretsbury Sports and Social Club, St Margarets. Do look in on us there – we meet on Thursday evenings from 8 pm. In recent years the club has benefited from generous sponsorship by the Cheshunt firm of Dobsons, whose Managing Director is an active member of the club.

Other Cycling Clubs

There are several other clubs in the county. If you wish to make contact but do not know of a local club, write to the Secretary of the British Cycling Federation at 36, Rockingham Road, Kettering, Northants. The Cyclists' Touring Club also has an active District Association. Details can be obtained from the National Secretary of the CTC at Cotterell House, 69 Meadrow, Godalming, Surrey GU7 3HS.